WILLIAM STILL

Wm Still

WILLIAM STILL:

HIS LIFE AND WORK TO THIS TIME.

———

BY JAMES P. BOYD

———

PHILADELPHIA:

WILLIAM STILL, Publisher,

224 SOUTH TWELFTH STREET

1886

REPUBLISHED BY:

SOUTH JERSEY CULTURE & HISTORY CENTER

2017

This edition published 2017 by the South Jersey Culture &
History Center at Stockton University

South Jersey Culture & History Center
Stockton University
101 Vera King Farris Drive
Galloway, New Jersey, 08205

Title: William Still: His Life and Work to This Time
Author: Boyd, James P.

Extracted from *STILL'S Underground Rail Road Records.
Revised Edition* (Philadephia: William Still, Publisher, 244
South Twelfth Street, 1886).

ISBN-13: 978-0-9976699-5-4

CONTENTS

FOREWORD

As a descendant of Levin and Charity Still, I have been recounting my family's history since the age of thirteen. William Still, the subject of this biography, was my third great granduncle, the youngest brother of my direct ancestor, Samuel Still. My third great grandfather, Samuel Still, was born February 7, 1805. As a young man, I grew up attending the various Still family history days throughout southern New Jersey. My father tasked me with cutting the grass and tending to Dr. James Still's gravesite behind Jacob's Chapel in Mount Laurel, Burlington County, and researching Still family documents. We spent many afternoons hiking through the Pine Barrens, with my father always pointing out places where my ancestors lived: the trails to the cedar swamps and cranberry bogs around the homestead of Levin and Charity Still in Shamong, New Jersey. My father was one of the last Levin and Charity descendants who actually dwelt on the familial homestead in Shamong.

Since the 1980s, with the resurgence of African Americans tracing their ancestry as a result of Alex Haley publishing his monumental work, *Roots*, black families have attempted to make historic connections to their families. As we gathered at various Still family reunions, primarily held in Mount Laurel, Lawnside and Vineland, New Jersey, most of us just assumed that we all descended from Levin and Charity Still. I recall discussions with my father and other family elders concerning Levin's original surname of "Steel." They quietly chided me to not concern myself with that information. Thirty years later, I began my journey in earnest of fact checking my family's history. In the past, some writers have regurgitated unfounded fakelore such as William, James, and Peter Still all resided in Snowhill (Lawnside), New Jersey, negating *in toto* the fact that they lived in Shamong. A list of children born to Levin and Charity Still found among the Peter Still papers records only fourteen births and not the eighteen Dr. James Still suggests in his book, *Early Recollections and Life of Dr. James Still*. False accounts indicate that the four unnamed children somehow reached their majority and settled in other places in New Jersey and some of same stories state that Levin Still was a descendent of the Guinea Prince. It appears no Still family members have ever conducted research to confirm or refute these assertions. Other fakelore place Levin's youngest son, William, in Camden, New Jersey, but, in reality, he moved from Shamong to Philadelphia, Pennsylvania, in 1844, where he resided for the remainder of his life. All of this fakelore has become "truth" to many people. For me, however, too many missing facts never permitted me to make the necessary connections.

In 2010 I began dissecting all the material I could find on my family's history. I wanted to delve deeper than what I observed on the surface. I began fact checking the fact checkers as other Still family members began discussing with me the pitfalls of the wider familial connections. Some said they could not find any linkage to Levin and Charity Still's progeny; many were frustrated by not finding the necessary associations and some just accepted the status quo. I queried the family historians and then fact checked their information. Why? Because all the "facts" provided did not add up. Everything was not as clean and simple as some historians or griots stated. I read a book that family historian Lurey Khan wrote, which stated that my fourth Great Grandfather's original surname was "Steel" prior to settling in New Jersey. I found this fact to be true, but I wanted to find more information and learn about Levin Steel and his family from Maryland's Eastern Shore. So why did Levin choose the name "Still" and not "Johnson," "Bustill" or "Smith"? Were all the Stills living in New Jersey and the surrounding areas blood related? What was the connection? When Levin made the trek to New Jersey, was he visiting other family members who had also escaped that peculiar institution of slavery and settled in Jersey? I was always amazed that no one around me really had conducted research or, if they did, failed to tell me about it. What about this man, Saunders Griffin, the purported white slave master of Levin and/or Sidney? What about Levin's wife Sidney (aka Charity) Still? Was she really on the same plantation with Levin? What about her family? I entertained so many questions, but I was sure clues existed that would point me to the truth. I wanted to travel and perform my own research, but where to start with so many unanswered questions?

I began dissecting the facts and checking historian's references by visiting various state archives. I posted parts of my research on social media. I wanted to start a conversation with other family members. Fortunately for me, a professional historian named Paul W. Schopp, who specializes in New Jersey and African American historical research, took notice of my posts. He approached me one day and said that he greatly appreciated my efforts on family research and that he found it refreshing that someone from the Still family was asking the hard questions and researching the facts. We soon developed a kinship through our mutual love of history. We would spend hours discussing our fact-finding adventures and would theorize where we should look next for more information.

One day my friend Paul asked me if I had read William Still's *The Underground Rail Road Records*, second edition, published in 1886. He noted the work contained an extensive biography of William by James P. Boyd. He felt it would provide me with some significant insights into William Still and my family's early beginnings. Boyd's perspective of William Still's familial origins, his personal life, his business, his marriage and his children imparted great insights to me and who I am as a person. It provided me with clues of Levin and Sidney Steel's life. It has helped me resolve some of the mysteries about my family history. I wanted to know more about Levin as an enslaved African. So with clues from Boyd's biography of William, along with some other clues from some remote historical abstract notes and a few theories of our own, Paul and I traveled several times to state and county archives in Maryland.

In the Boyd biography, William noted that his mother remained in slavery under Saunders Griffin. That was a mystery for a long time because no person by that name existed in the federal census records or in all the county and state records. Paul theorized that Saunders could be a nickname for Alexander and that his last name wasn't Griffin but Griffith. We discovered that there was an Alexander

Griffith who owned a substantial plantation in Caroline County, Maryland, along with several enslaved Africans. We discovered that Levin and Sidney were on the same plantation in Caroline County for a time but not the one belonging to Saunders Griffith. Rather, William Banning owned both Levin and Sidney as young children. After William Banning's death in May 8, 1780, his will devised Levin to his widow, Margaret Banning. William devised Sidney to his daughter, Lydia Morton, who apparently later sold Sidney to Alexander Griffith. Margaret Banning died soon after her late husband and, in her last will and testament, she devised to her young grandson, William Wood, "a negro boy named Levin." Boyd reports in his biography of William Still that Levin and his owner were about the same age. William Wood soon became an orphan and his guardian filed yearly accounts in the Caroline County Orphan Court. These records revealed the costs involved in maintaining Levin and that he worked and earned money for William Wood.

Through research, we met and befriended other historians and researchers who assisted us in our quest. A chance meeting with Dr. Clara Small, a former professor at Salisbury State University, who, through her research, located Levin Steel's manumission or freedom papers in the Maryland land records, provided irrefutable evidence that he purchased his freedom on November 22, 1798. Prior to 1810, freedom papers of most enslaved Africans were recorded in deed books because, as most should understand, slaves were considered property and property transactions were recorded in deed books. Did Levin Steel have other family members in Maryland Eastern Shore? We know that there are several "Steel" family members that resided on the Eastern Shore. Do they have familial connections to Levin Steel?

We cannot ignore the fact that Levin Steel deliberately assumed the name "Still"; it is a significant point. Manumission research revealed several Still family members residing in nearby Evesham Township and that they received their freedom papers prior to 1805, the year Levin arrived in Burlington County. We know that the Still family was present in New Jersey as far back as 1752, when a Delilah Still was born. The family's presence in South Jersey probably extends back to the opening years of the eighteenth century or even into the late seventeenth century. Levin must have met or even befriended some members of the Still family and felt comfortable enough to assume the name "Still" as his new surname. By changing his surname from Steel to Still, which has little distinction aurally, Levin essentially grafted himself and his progeny into the original New Jersey Still family, who were thriving all throughout southern New Jersey. Even after he made this deliberate and conscious decision, however, he painstakingly thought about where to settle, finally choosing to live in the desolate secluded area of the Pine Barrens near the Old Brotherton Indian Reservation.

What about the history of the original southern New Jersey Still family and its progeny? We know much about them from the nineteenth century forward to today, but what made them so significant prior to the nineteenth century? Where did the name "Still" come from? Was it a plantation owner's last name given to their newly freed Africans? Our research has not found any historical record of a large plantation owner with the surname "Still" in New

Jersey or surrounding area. Did the surname derive from the occupation in which these enslaved Africans engaged, a common practice during the sixteenth and seventeenth century?

At the turn of the nineteenth century, only a smattering of small black enclaves existed across South Jersey's landscape, including the settlements of Snowhill and Guineatown. By the mid 1820s, however, the number of discreet communities for African American—both free and fugitive—had proliferated, due in part to the 1804 New Jersey Gradual Manumission Act. Many of these communities provided residential shelter for locally manumitted people of color, while a small select number of these settlements exclusively offered fugitive slaves a place of relative safety: communities like Timbuctoo, Kenilworth, Free Haven and Marshalltown. The enclaves established for local blacks often had Still families residing in them. We know that the Religious Society of Friends (Quakers) played a significant role in assisting fugitive enslaved Africans to hide and resettle in New Jersey, as did the African Methodist Episcopal Church and its envoys.

There are many mysteries yet to be solved. Much research remains to be conducted in county archives, land and property transactions, old newspapers, church records and various manuscript collections, to aid in unlocking stories of the Still family that lived in New Jersey long prior to Levin Steel settling out in the Pines. Many years ago, I attended a history program at Temple University and heard the Underground Railroad historian, Charles Blockson, speak. Something he said has stayed with me to this day; to paraphrase, we should stop regurgitating the history that is already known and start researching and telling the stories of our ancestors that have not been told.

As African Americans, many of the connections to our original culture have been buried or lost to us. But our significance to building America is all around us and it is important for us to research it, discover it and tell it. It is important to know from whence we come and that our enslaved African ancestors were not just uneducated slaves, but survivors.

Boyd's biography of William Still has been invaluable and an inspiration to my research. It is my hope that others are inspired in the same way by reading this work. I am very pleased that the South Jersey Culture & History Center at Stockton University has taken on this project of reprinting Boyd's interview with William Still. I want to say thanks to Paul W. Schopp, Dr. Clara Small, Dr. Thomas Kinsella and the small army of volunteers at the Dr. James Still Historic Site and Education Center for their encouragement and support. I must also especially thank my wife, Kym Still, for allowing me to spend time away from home researching, proofreading, and listening to me vent about my journey on my family blood trail through history.

Be inspired!

> Samuel C. Still III
> Chairman
> Dr. James Still Historic Site and Education Center
> Medford, New Jersey

WILLIAM STILL

For many years the friends of William Still have desired to see a sketch of his life in print. The propriety of a memoir has been repeatedly urged in connection with his Underground Railroad records. General Armstrong has warmly pressed him to furnish a biographical account of himself for the columns of the *Southern Workman*. Other editors and educators, white and colored, have often expressed a kindred wish.

He has not been unmindful of the compliment conveyed in these often requests, but business cares have so engrossed his thoughts and occupied his time that he has not, thus far, found it possible to comply with them. And, though contrary to the good old adage, it may be that, in this instance, delay has not proved dangerous.

It will be accepted as true that, so far as the colored race is concerned, time has vindicated postponement by multiplying possible readers, and, doubtless, too, by increasing their ability to understand and appreciate. Moreover, the preparation of a new edition of the Underground Railroad records seems to offer an opportunity never before presented for the publication of such a sketch as has been in request. Those records have already been largely read by the colored people of the South, and it is very probable they will be still more largely read by them, in view of the fact that they present so many quaint, curious, yet authentic, chapters of a history which most intimately concerns them, but which would never have become accessible to them nor the general public had its data not been carefully preserved and published by Mr. Still.

It might, therefore, serve to gratify a rational curiosity to see, in connection with them, an account of the author's life. And we doubt not it would be counted as pardonable pride on his part to wish, at this opportune moment, that his personal history might go out with his work. But these make a low plane on which to move. Other and higher motives exist for such publication of his life as is now attempted.

Be it known he does not seek through the medium of this sketch to make himself conspicuous in any way. He is a modest man, and content with the quiet, unworded favor of his kind. But there is an example in his life, and he does seek, as every good man does, to set a lesson before the colored people of America which, even if they do not learn it by heart, may serve to acquaint them with the possibilities within their reach and encourage them to do that for themselves which none outside of themselves can do.

William Still has seen his race bowed and broken by slavery. He has contributed the best years of his life to a cause which loosened their chains and wiped the blot of man-ownership and involuntary servitude from our institutions. That crisis passed, that event an achievement, he sees them in the midst of a problem whose solution is far more difficult.

They could not contribute much directly to the cause of freedom. Their yoke was too heavy and too securely fixed. Their hands were shackled. Their minds were clouded. Their ambitions were blunted. They could not grasp situations, save as a child reaches vacantly for the moon. And not much was expected of them. The moral forces at work outside of them, the political forces clashing high over them, the physical forces playing somewhat in their midst, and of which they at last got to be a part, these were the agencies which came to their rescue and made the chattels men.

But now what of the problem? They are men; yet in servitude to themselves, as all men are; slaves to a situation; serfs to surroundings. Now no moral forces outside of themselves can avail them much. Now no political forces can contend for mastery over their heads, for they are, or ought to be, a part of them. Now no physical forces can cleave chains, break barriers and shift situations except those in their own hands.

True, they invite, and will ever have, sympathy. True, they deserve, and will ever receive, encouragement. But both sympathy and encouragement will be in direct ratio to the proofs they give of ability to serve and lift themselves. The chains are off the slaves, but the solemn, hard responsibilities of life are on the freedmen. Are they equal to the task, nay, the duty, of self-emancipation? Can they grow into factors of our institutions, as important as their numbers? Can they organize industries and achieve wealth? Can they climb up out of menial valleys on to the table land of mechanics and artizanship? Can they build and control schools? Can they formulate and maintain codes, political, social, moral and religious? Can they learn to do whatever white men of right do, and to be as influential and useful, in the midst of modern civilization, as white men are?

Full of faith that the race need not, for all time, be an exceptional one on account of its color and previous enslaved condition, and that it can and will, under proper encouragement and with the gradually growing confidence which comes from favorable trials and accumulated experience, answer all these questions in the affirmative, we open for them the lesson, indeed the many lessons, found in the life and work of our subject, with a view to helping them in their upward march.

What one of their number has done, under circumstances quite as adverse as any to be met with now or in the future, without regard to section, any other of their number or all may do. Wherein one by his pluck and perseverance has overcome poverty, illiteracy, prejudice, has made for himself a large, growing, and profitable business, has become a useful and influential member of society, any other or all can do it. Not in degree, perhaps, yet in kind, and that is all that is needed; for the colored race, like any other, will be judged by its possibilities and achievements as a race, and not by the failure of any one of its members to acquire as much wealth or attain as high a distinction as another.

PARENTAGE AND EARLY LIFE

Years on years ago, when slavery was strongly intrenched in church and state, when the sentiment against it was neither widespread nor pronounced, when all its hard and odious laws prescribing title in man and woman, regulating their purchase and safe-keeping, and providing for their recovery in case they ran away, were as easily and readily enforced as any other laws, there lived a slave family on the eastern shore of Maryland whose husband and father could not acquiesce in the righteousness of bondage.

He was a young man who had felt the brutality of mastership. His back had been almost broken by a maul in the hands of a cruel master or overseer. The authority that should have protected had maimed him. The burden of life, which was not easily borne by even the strongest, was thus made harder for him. How could he help resenting an ownership which lacked a kindness not withheld from the lower animals? How could he help detesting a mastery which harshly exacted, yet in a spirit of savagery made the victim incapable of responding to exaction?

This slave, his wife and children, and the entire population of the negro quarters, passed by descent from an old to a young master. The rivets which fastened their manacles were not broken by the death of the former owner, but held as securely under the new. The land, the cattle, the slaves—things inanimate, things living and without souls, things living and with souls—passed, in obedience to inexorable law, from sire to son.

With perceptions quickened by a transition which showed how title in man could, without his consent, be so fixed as to pass to a successor, and with full recollection of the previous brutal mastery, the young slave resolved to free himself from the legal conditions which bound alike the stones of the field, the beasts of the stall, and the members of his race. He made known his intentions to his young master. Parleying was of but little worth, for the slave had meditated long and resolved like a Spartan. His final overture was very much as if he had said, "Give me liberty, or give me death!" The fact that it took the humbler form of, "Massa, I'd sooner die than stay a slave," robs it of none of its heroism.

The young master doubtless saw that it would be impossible to change the determination of the slave, and felt that it would be policy under the circumstances to drive the best bargain he could. So, on reflection, he determined to sell him to himself, or in other words to give him a chance to buy his freedom. A price was named which was low in comparison with the prices of a later period, and it was accepted by the slave. His former diligence was now doubly taxed to complete the hard task of working out his freedom. Opportunities for making overtime and over-money were infrequent, but by dint of perseverance and economy he succeeded, and the coveted boon of freedom was his reward.

This once slave but now freeman was Levin Steel— afterwards changed to Still, the better to escape identity by Southern claimants and pursuers of his family. Being free, he could not breathe an air tainted by slavery, nor brook the surroundings of bondage. So, severing the sacred ties of family, bidding good-bye to his wife, Cidney, and the four children she had borne him—two boys and two girls—and trusting under God to a future which should be brighter for himself and loved ones than the past, he started North, and located in the neighborhood of Greenwich, New Jersey.

The bereft wife felt more keenly than ever the weight of her yoke. She too resolved to lift and break it, but not in the tedious, painstaking way her husband had done. She would, for the sake of liberty and reunion, accept the trials and dangers of escape, and, if need be, the death which such an attempt often involved. For days and weeks she wrestled with the problem. For herself alone it would have been a simple one, but every plan was complicated by the presence of her children. How could she rescue them also? At last a scheme was perfected. Under the influence of her mighty resolution, hopeful of such indirect aid as her husband could furnish, trusting to that Providence which made the way of the wilderness plain, she set out on her toilsome, fugitive journey. Then came days made harrowing by waiting and watching and fear of detection, nights perilous with forced travel, times of despair as swamp and forest interposed, rivers intervened, or starvation threatened. All the tribulations of an ordinary escape were intensified a hundred-fold as she secretly pushed her way Northward, weighted with care for her four children.

Success crowned her perils and sacrifices. The father's heart and hand had been diligent in her movements, as she had anticipated. The severed family were joyfully reunited. An abode was provided near Greenwich. The old name of Steel became Still, and every precaution was taken to preserve the secret of their past existence, and establish a new identity which should be to them a protection.

But the scent of the slave-hunter was not to be baffled by these precautions. The trail was run, if not rapidly, yet unerringly, and in a few months the New Jersey hiding place was discovered. A capturing gang, terrible as an "army with banners," suddenly pounced upon the peaceful household, and the wife and four children were dragged back to their old slave-quarters on the Eastern Shore.

Liberty's draught once tasted, the lips of the slave mother longed for it again. More than ever, escape would prove hard and dangerous. Still her thoughts were never vacant of plans for a second attempt. None seemed feasible which embraced her four children, the two eldest of which were boys, Levin and Peter, aged respectively six and eight years, the two youngest being girls, mere infants. Agonizing as was the thought of severing her children and leaving a part of them behind, perhaps never to be seen again, she could not overcome the dreadful alternative by any ingenuity of hers. Her own dear mother was there and in bondage. She, at least, would be a friend and protector of those left behind. Here was a ray of comfort amid the great cloud of agony; something to reconcile a maternal heart to a surrender sadder than that of death and burial.

So a plan was at last worked out. She would leave the boys, the oldest and strongest. What tears watered the sad compulsion! She would save the girls, the youngest and weakest. Angel-approved are a mother's holy instincts! The sorrowful night came. Nerved for the hour and the solemn occasion, she rushed to the little straw bed on which her four were sleeping, kissed her boys farewell without waking them, clasped the two little girls in her strong, true arms, bade her mother good-bye, and trusting in God, began again the perilous march for freedom. Of the trials met, hardships overcome, and dangers avoided, we will not make a twice-told tale. She reached the free soil of Jersey, and rejoined her husband with her precious charge.

Now greater precaution was necessary to elude pursuit and avoid discovery. The old abode was not to be thought of. A home was selected in the depth of the Jersey pines in Burlington county, about seven miles to the east of Medford. In this sequestered spot the father became an owner of about forty acres of land. The neighborhood was thinly settled by people mostly poor, who subsisted by small farming, wood chopping, charcoal burning, marl digging, cranberry picking and the like. The life of his surroundings became the life of Levin Still. Carefully guarding his family history, working peaceably and industriously, dealing honestly, walking reverently, he was permitted to escape the pursuit of the slave hunter, and to enjoy, as much as circumstances would allow, the blessings of freedom. His acres became his own. Thrift brought its reward to him as to other men. His family increased till it numbered eighteen children in all, the youngest of whom was William Still, the subject of our sketch.

He was born October 7th, 1821. When old enough, he began to work on the farm, on which was raised corn, rye, potatoes, and other vegetables. The farming stock consisted

23

of a horse and a yoke of oxen. The farm help—the father and several stalwart sons—was quite out of proportion to the acres and the stock. Other avenues of labor had to be sought. They were readily found in the surrounding pines, the cedar swamps, the cranberry meadows, and the harvest fields, within a radius of seven to ten miles. Into these all the boys, as they grew older, entered. It was nothing unusual for the Still boys to put up hundreds of cords of wood in a single winter. At an early age William was an expert at chopping. Wishing to show his skill one day, he cut and put up one cord of market wood before 12 o'clock, noon. A wealthy merchant by the name of Samuel Fennimore, residing at Lumberton, complimented him for this feat by saying "he had never seen it done before by a boy under sixteen," and to show his appreciation he rewarded him with a half dollar, which was thankfully received.

A few miles from his home were the "Cedar Swamps." Thither the boys often went to cut and prepare the class of timber which grew there for the market. In the proper season, they were wont to go to the celebrated Atzion Cranberry Meadows, five or six miles south. These meadows invited quite a number of promiscuous pickers, and as there were no restrictions in those days, they were a source of profit to all who chose to engage in the industry. They were owned by Samuel Richards, who carried on the foundry business in Atzion, but whose residence was in Philadelphia.

Seven miles westward lay Medford. It was the centre of a rich agricultural section, mostly populated by thrifty Quakers. This town was the chief trading point for the people of the pines. Thither they carried their farm products, hauled their wood, and other commodities, and after exchanging them for groceries, marl, lime, and the like, the same made up their home or back load. Among these farmers the boys were always sure of a long harvest period, kind treatment, and good wages. Regularly they availed themselves of the opportunity thus presented. Industry was the rule in the house of the elder Still, and the training of the children had been such that they were particularly proud of the reports they carried back from the harvest field. To this pride must be attributed an early resolution on the part of William, which he has never broken, and which contributed as much as any one thing could, to his healthful age, moral standing, and business success. Whiskey was served, according to custom, to the harvest hands. One day William, oppressed by the heat and his efforts to do a full hand's work—a task for which he was quite too young—was induced to take a drink. It sickened him, and incapacitated him for further service, so that he was forced to return home and report a quarter of a day's lost labor. Thus humiliated, he resolved never to touch the accursed stuff again. If there is anything in his life of which he is proud, it is the faithful keeping of the vow then registered.

His recollection of these old Quaker families for whom he used to harvest, and from whom he received many kindnesses, is vivid and pleasant. They numbered, among others, the Reeves, Stokes, Haines, Wilkinses, Braddocks, Ballingers, Shreeves, Hollingsheads, Evans, Doughtons and Fennimores, all intelligent, substantial people, and many of them closely identified with that great movement which culminated in the freedom of the slave race.

Equally well he remembers the denizens of the pines, who were his more immediate neighbors. Among them were the Smalls, Cranes, Leyallens, Minjins, Smiths, Browns, Pipers, Millers, McCamerons, McNeals, Moores and Wellses, who, if not favored with much wealth and education, were yet a sturdy, independent people, with all the characteristics of the pioneer. Close by his home dwelt an Indian family by the name of Moore. It was the dwindled remains of the last Indian tribe that inhabited Southern New Jersey. The members made their living by fishing, basket-making, etc. There too was the old "Injin Mill," on the site of what was once the "Injin Town."

It was at the house of one Thomas Wilkins, an old bachelor, that an incident occurred which served to fix indelibly on William's youthful mind the atrocious character of the slave system. Mr. Wilkins' immediate household consisted of himself and two aged sisters. He had in his employ a great, strong, resolute colored man who had run away from bondage, and who had made up his mind never to be captured alive. His master's gang tracked him to his hiding-place, and one dark, rainy night a colored decoy rapped at the door, saying he had a message to deliver to the slave, which could only be delivered in person. Suspiciously and reluctantly the slave came down and cautiously opened the door. As soon as it was ajar the gang rushed in and, knowing the strength and resolution of their victim, pounced upon him with bludgeon and fist to disable him. The encounter was terrific. Not until the poor fellow was beaten almost to a jelly did he succumb. The hand-cuffs were securely fastened on one wrist, and as they were about to lock them on the other, Mr. Wilkins and his two sisters came to the scene. Without weapon of any kind, aged and frightened almost out of their wits, one of them seized the fire shovel, ran it into the coals which had been covered for the night, and threw a shovelful of glow-ing embers into the midst of the assailants. This created a temporary panic. The slave was quick to take advantage of the moment. Laying about him, with the handcuff for a weapon, he turned the panic of the gang to flight. Fear-ing a second attempt at rescue, it was deemed prudent to change his quarters at once. Aid was sought, and it fell to the lot of William and his brother-in-law, Gabriel Thomp-son, to pilot him to a place of greater safety. Dark and rainy as the night was they took the slave, all cut about the head and body and bleeding profusely, in charge, and escorted him through deep pine forest and intricate road-way, a distance of some twenty miles, to the vicinity of Egg Harbor, and then, wet to the skin, tired and footsore, they returned, reaching home the next morning.

As the reader may well guess, opportunities for schooling were very meagre among a people so sparse and primitive as those of the pines. A little schooling on rainy days was all William got till he was seventeen years old. This uncertain attendance barely enabled him to know how to read. The school was never very inviting, the teach-ers were none of the best, the branches taught were only the simplest, and worst of all, there was a strong prejudice existing among the scholars, and not unfrequently in the breast of teachers, against the colored pupils. This prejudice took many ingenious shapes—prejudice is always cowardly and ingenious. As an instance, one evening when the pupils were on their way home and were crossing a bridge, a crowd of them surged against William and pushed him over the edge into the water, which was about four feet deep. This and similar exhibitions of prejudice forced the teacher to dismiss the colored pupils in advance of the whites, in order that they might keep out of harm's way. At another time, for some real or imaginary offence, the teacher ornamented him with a pair of leather goggles and stood him out before the school, where he became the source of much merriment. His father happened in just then, and being a man of strong temper, ready to stand up for the rights of himself and children, there was quite a scene between him and the teacher, during which the latter entirely failed to give adequate reason or excuse for a punishment so exceptional and ridiculous. William, and all his brothers in attendance, were taken away from school, and the same teacher being in charge for three winters, no further opportunities for schooling were presented during that time.

Afterwards the old-fashioned desultory way of attending school on rainy days, and in the meantime going into the woods or prosecuting some other labor, was taken up and continued till William reached the age of seventeen. It happened then that a teacher was secured who was more favorably inclined to the colored race, or who could, at least, act impartially toward all his pupils. This was regarded as a golden opportunity. Dropping all other work, William went an entire quarter. The school was large, numbering some fifty-five pupils, old and young, and most of them not inclined to study much. The branches taught were of the primitive kind, never rising to the dignity of English Grammar. To say that he made any very great advance would be to overstate the truth. Yet he was an earnest pupil, fully determined to take advantage of the situation. He was at school by sunrise, and engaged in study long before the other pupils came. The hours of noon were similarly spent. After school, and as long as the teacher stayed he would bend his energies to his books. At spelling and definitions he became quite expert; so much so, that it was nothing unusual for him to repeat a whole column of words with their meanings, without requiring the teacher to give them out; and when a hard word passed the length of the spelling class, it was the custom of the teacher to turn it over to him for a final and correct orthography. Declamation was one of the exercises. In this he took great delight, and inasmuch as it was a terror to the rest of the pupils, he soon got the reputation of being about the only one who could go through on declamation day. He pursued arithmetic as found in Pike's old work, through "The Rules of Three," and as far as "Interest," copying all his sums, according to custom, into a blank book.

The next winter he got but four weeks' schooling, and this ended his career as a common school pupil. But what a wonderful transformation had come over his fellow-pupils! The prejudices against him, on account of color, were greatly allayed. He was no longer the subject of jeer and insult. Respect for the efforts he was making, and for his real acquisitions, took the place of taunt and scoff. This mattered much to him, for it showed that the sure and royal way of correcting prejudices against his race was to prove that, by blameless conduct and earnest application, it could achieve whatever the same characteristics achieved for the white or any other race.

What little rudimentary education he had thus far gotten would not count for much in these days of improved schools and larger facilities for learning, but it served to beget in him a desire for information of a wider and higher order. He became a great reader of such historical and geographical books as were accessible. A work called *The Young Man's Own Book* fell into his hands. This was read and re-read till he could repeat almost entire chapters of it. Its chapter on grammar induced him to buy one, and he pursued this branch while driving team, during leisure in the woods, and at nights by the light of the pine fire, when engaged in paring apples, shelling corn, and performing such tasks as were set the children during the long winter evenings.

About this time he subscribed for the *Colored American*, which, by the way, was edited by Charles B. Ray and Philip Bell, of New York, and was the first anti-slavery newspaper in this country owned and published by colored men. Abolitionists were odious in those days. The postmaster did not consider it altogether proper to dispense this kind of literature through the mails, and so, in the exercise of an arbitrary power, withheld William's paper for four or five weeks. At last, on one of his weekly calls at the office, he was informed that he could have his papers if he would pay what was due on them. On agreeing to do so, he was given a bundle of papers numbering about thirty copies, for which he paid thirty cents postage. When he got home and unfolded them they proved to be, with one or two exceptions, the old undelivered numbers of other papers than his own. He pocketed his disappointment, and called as before at the post-office to meet with better luck, the postmaster being satisfied with the glory, or having grown ashamed, of his shabby trick.

In the fall of 1841 William left home to try the world on his own account. He was nearing the age of manhood, and felt that there were larger opportunities for him outside of the "pent-up Utica" of the pines. He did not succeed in finding steady employment by the month, as was his intention, but had to content himself with job work, such as digging potatoes, husking corn and cutting wood. In the following spring, he engaged with Mr. Joshua Borton, at Evesham Mount, for the period of one year, at the rate of ten dollars per month, to do general farm work, and as his only steady hand. The farm consisted of about one hundred acres, the larger part cleared land, and, as Mr. Borton, who had been more closely engaged in carriage-building than in the pursuit of farming, was not himself a skilled farmer, William found plenty of work to do. He greatly enjoyed this new life, and felt proud of the responsibilities it thrust upon him. He had charge of the farm team and of the driving team of his employer. The laying out of the land for crops, the preparation of the ground, the sowing and the harvesting were almost entirely intrusted to him. He led the hands in the harvest-fields and was sent to market occasionally with produce, which he took much pains to dispose of at good prices, and to carefully return the moneys arising from the sales. It was a pleasant and profitable year to him. He was well treated by his employer, and he took great care not to abuse in any way the confidence he had voluntarily reposed in him. He still finds it a source of satisfaction, looking back to it, in that it was a successful trial of his ability to maintain himself and to bring into play a wider range of managing and business qualities than his home life permitted or required him to do. He stayed his year out, and left with some sixty or seventy dollars in hand.

During this year, on December 24, 1842, his father died. This affliction bore heavily on him and inclined him to serious thoughts respecting his moral condition and future well-being. The subtle workings of his mind, the monitions of quickened conscience, the progressions toward a change of heart, are matters best exemplified by his own account of them. He says: "I found myself painfully conscious of the fact that I had, up to that time, turned a deaf ear to the 'still small voice' which had so often admonished me to 'seek first the kingdom of God and his righteousness'; that I had walked after the imagination of my old, sinful heart, contrary to the counsel of the Light of the world, Christ, and that, in my blindness and unbelief, I had rejected the proffered salvation of Christ, preferring to follow the voice of the stranger who was seducing me from God and Heaven. Mournfully brooding over my situation, and with no expectation of a speedy relief, I went one morning to the woods—a distance of several miles—with the team. The ground and trees were all covered with snow. The sun shone out brightly, and soon the snow began to melt before his rays. To my amazement, my load of sorrow began of a sudden to leave me, to melt away, as it were, like the snow before the sun. Streams of joy, peace and gratitude overflowed my heart. I felt that the wonderful Providence that had wrought in me such a radical change was entitled to my thanksgiving and praise while I lived. Never before in my experience or conception had I approached such a transition. Even the lonely woods and chilly snow seemed pervaded with loveliness and a source of indescribable cheer. I felt that it was the heart's deliverance which appropriately followed my previous mental surrender to the great Ruler and my recorded resolve to seek his kingdom, taking the Sermon on the Mount as my guide and inspiration.

"In 1843 the lectures of Father Miller (as he was called) on the Second Coming of Christ fell into my hands, and were read with great interest. I never before had had my mind awakened to the idea of any literal reign or restitution. I therefore resolved to read whatever I could find in the Bible and out of it bearing on the Second Coming. In doing so I was struck with the seeming harmony which existed between the great Book and the doctrines of those who discussed the subject. I felt that, however variant opinions were, or whatever was said, He must come. No part of the Bible had such an influence in determining my convictions as Matthew, chapter 24. Nevertheless, I never got so far as to believe that any man was infallible, nor that any one understood all there was in the Scriptures, nor that, if the predicted time of the coming failed, I was to have no faith in the Bible, but I was persuaded, rather, that 'neither death, nor life, nor angels, nor principalities, nor things present, nor things to come, nor powers, nor height, nor depth, nor any other creature, should separate us from the love of God which is in Christ.' So when 1843-4 passed, my faith and hope remained unchanged in the All-Supreme."

HIS REMOVAL TO PHILADELPHIA

Persuaded that city life would afford him better opportunities for such mental improvement as he desired, as well as for business success, than the country, he left New Jersey, in the spring of 1844, and came to Philadelphia. His cash in hand did not exceed three dollars; his wardrobe was meagre, of city friends and counsellors he had none; but he had better stock in trade than these, made up of steady, well-grounded habits, a good, stout heart, and a desire to succeed on the only sure basis of perseverance, economy and integrity. Philadelphia was not as great then as to-day, but there was sufficient about its throng of people, its street mazes, its business hurly-burly, its uncertainties of home, place and occupation, to daze, if not unman, a simple country youth, unused to other noises than the low of cattle, and other intricacies than the twisting by-paths through the Jersey pine forests.

Be it known the question of color had to be confronted also. He knew what this meant amid his rural surroundings, for he had battled with it, and, as we have seen, successfully. But now it would present itself under new phases. How could he meet them? Would they tie and hamper him so that the same laws of success which controlled white men would not operate in his favor? Would his life in the metropolis be, on account of his color, a mere privation and discipline, with no progress, no influence, no substantial result, to speak in behalf of industry pursued, economy exercised, integrity cultivated and applied? Could he, in his new estate, and despite all obstacles, mould himself a man and establish himself as a useful factor amid urban surroundings? These were momentous questions, which he could not answer then. But he knew that time would answer them. So, indulging the faith that honorable exertion must wear her crown, without respect to race, he sought an abode.

This he found on Fifth street above Poplar. It was an old frame shanty, of rickety construction and slim proportion, yet it sufficed to bar the weather, and was quite as palatial as his limited means and uncertain prospects enabled him to afford. It could scarcely be called urban, for it was quite adjacent to commons, corn-fields, potato-patches, and brick-yards.

His first experience in city life after securing a home was not very well calculated to favorably impress a youth who had known nothing but the quietude of the country. The Native American agitation was at its height. Deep, volcanic rumblings were heard everywhere. Soon the fires burst forth, and enveloped the entire city. Law was silent in the presence of the mob. The police were helpless. For forty-eight hours the Native American adherents, promiscuously armed, rushed infuriately about the streets, attacking the Catholic supporters, scarcely less in numbers, similarly armed, and just as infuriate and blood-thirsty. The clash was terrifically brutal and murderous. Many Catholic churches and other valuable properties were burned. The large church of that denomination, then in course of erection at the corner of Fifth street and Girard avenue, and within almost a stone-throw of William's stopping-place, was fired by the mob, and only escaped total destruction through the vigilance of the firemen.

It became necessary to bring a stronger power than the police to bear on the rioters. The military were called out, and battle took the place of indiscriminate violence. The mob wheeled cannon into line and confronted the soldiery. There was stubborn resistance, mutual firing of musketry and ordnance, charge and counter-charge, great bloodshed and loss of life. There was an encampment of soldiers on the common in front of William's home, and for three days a battle impended in that locality. At any moment he might have found himself in the midst of a battle-scene, with his house riddled by bullets or knocked to pieces by cannon balls. Notwithstanding his jeopardy, he stuck to his humble quarters till law triumphed and peace reigned. But he never credited this adhesiveness more to absolute bravery than to the rather compelling fact that he did not know where to go to in case he left his home.

This agitation over, and safety of person and life assured, he must seek employment. Where? At what? There was one popular avenue open, that of waiting; but, though light work, he had no knowledge of it, and no inclination to engage in it. It was to him a life of dependence, with no outcome in it. Looking beyond this, he applied at a brick-yard in the month of April. Being unused to that kind of work, and unable to give any guarantee of ability to perform it, he failed to secure a place. However, it so happened that in one of the yards there was a very steep wheeling-ground, which was shunned by experienced laborers. There an opening offered, which, hard as the task was, he agreed to fill. He held his place till the end of the season, and quit with a little extra cash in hand on account of the difficulty of the wheel. Feeling that he had done quite well, considering the price paid for labor, which was much less than now, he began to look about for other employment.

Now he met with much discouragement, and failure became a source of great anxiety, for winter was approaching—his first winter away from home, and in a great, friendless city. Turn which way he would, the avenues were full. In anxious search, he fell in with an old gentleman whose garb bespoke him a Quaker, who offered to engage him to thresh clam-shells by the cart-load. The shells were to be threshed into powder for some unknown purpose. Unmindful of Don Quixote's battle with the wind-mills, or the peasant's attempt to gather wool by shearing a pig, he jumped at the old friend's proposal, and went speedily and enthusiastically to work, without being very particular about terms. For two days he worked industriously, when it began to dawn on him that threshing clam-shells with a flail was truly a "labor in vain," for an examination proved that he was not hurting the shells very much, and that they were stubbornly resisting his most earnest attempts to reduce them to powder. Though he had accepted the job on the principle that "a half loaf is better than no bread," he foresaw that to continue this work further would be to postpone indefinitely all prospects of obtaining even the coveted half loaf. So he quit rather unceremoniously, and smothered his chagrin over lost time and labor by looking for other work.

A man by the name of Shanklin, who stood on the wharf and made a living by hauling wood and other things, offered to let him drive one of his carts on the shares. This offer was accepted. Some days a job of hauling was had, other days none. After a few weeks' trial of this work he found he was not making enough to pay even his very modest board-bill. Other fields must therefore be tried. Nothing permanent offered, but several temporary jobs fell in his way, by means of which he was enabled to pass the winter.

In the spring he went back to his old place in the brick-yard, where he stayed the season through, quitting with a little money ahead, as before. Then came the question of passing a second winter in the city. He wished to avoid the struggle of the previous winter, and thought to start a business of his own. Menial work was hard, but for this he did not care so much as for the fact that it was difficult to obtain and of uncertain tenure. Moreover, it did not give him the opportunity for mental improvement he desired, and it stunted rather than encouraged his ambition to be something else than a mere "hewer of wood and drawer of water" for others. There was a sense of independence about a business of his own, which he wished to enjoy as soon as he could strike something suitable.

But here came up the old questions, what? where? He had no business experience except that derived from a brief service in a stove store on Second street, and from frequent errands to an oyster-cellar kept by an old colored man, who was quite noted for his excellent stews and unrivalled pepper-pot. The latter business might do. It was worth trying, if for no other reason because it best suited his limited capital. Accordingly, a cellar was procured on Second street, and he embarked in the oyster business. The rush of customers he fondly anticipated did not come along. He found it wasn't the business he imagined it to be, and that in order to capture custom he must keep open till after the theatres were out and the night-prowler had become real hungry, and even then he wasn't sure of patronage unless he engaged to dispense something a little stronger than oyster broth, which he was totally unwilling to do.

A very brief experience assured him that he was not fit for the business, or the business for him; and that prudence demanded of him to quit. His exit was hastened by a plausible fellow of comely proportion, dignified manner and excellent speech, who passed himself off as a member of the Baptist church and a pronounced friend of the colored race. This fellow, after completely enlisting his sympathy by his plausible talk and pious assumptions, succeeded in borrowing of him nearly all his working capital, on the pretext that the loan was only for his temporary accommodation and that the money would be returned inside of an hour. For this feature of the business he had made no provision. His design of quitting voluntarily now became compulsory. Prospective profit had become real loss. Antic-ipated success had turned out disaster. He withdrew, with the credit side of his book almost a blank, except where he made cautious entry of experience gained, and care-fully noted the comfort derived from a well-learned lesson.

Not despondent, he cast about for other ventures. A colored friend, engaged as porter in a store, suggested that he could furnish an abundance of second-hand clothing, if he, William, would engage to sell them. Having his vacant cellar on hand he thought it might be turned to account in this way. In a twinkle he became a second-hand clothes-dealer, and felt that fickle fortune could not much longer restrain her coming. But he was disillusioned even more quickly than before. The promising combination got ajar in three days' time. He had escaped Scylla only to fall into Charybdis. His first venture was an approach to bankruptcy; this was a plunge directly into it. One week settled the matter, and left him adrift and moneyless just on the eve of winter.

The situation was somewhat desperate. He had his disappointments to pocket and his energies to recuperate for a trial which want made imperative. Fortunately, a gentleman was building several houses near his boarding place. His urgent application for work was rewarded by a contract to dig three wells and grade the yards. This work ended in mid-winter. He strove harder than ever to find other employment, but failed. Labor had gone into winter quarters along with the people. In sheer desperation, he turned his thoughts toward an avocation he had always detested—that of waiting. Looking over the columns of the *Ledger*, he found "wants" in profusion, accompanied by flattering offers of pay. Hastening to an Intelligence office, as directed by the advertisement, he deposited a dollar, had his name recorded, and was given a slip of paper with directions to go to a certain place where his services would be commanded. He found he was not wanted there at all. Here was discomfiture and mystery. When light dawned, it looked very much as if the Intelligence impostor had resorted to a contemptible trick to fleece him of a dollar.

Watching the papers further, but with little hope, he finally saw that a waiter was wanted at the Broad Street House. Applying personally, he got the situation, and a shabby enough one it was. The landlord was a Pennsylvania Dutchman, and his guests came mostly from Reading and thereabouts. The pay was to be the magnificent sum of $5 per month, with the perquisite of an occasional glass of beer, which latter remuneration was never accepted. There was plenty of work, late and early, but the surroundings were disgusting. The worst feature of all was his bed, which was a pallet of straw under the stairs, upon which he crawled very much as a dog enters its kennel. His first night on that wretched apology for a bed was a sad one. He could not help thinking that, after all, the boasted comfort of city life was but a glamour, and that his humble lot among the Jersey pines was luxurious in comparison with this. As visions of his once happy home and cosy nesting-place arose, he could not restrain his tears. However, he bade heroism to the rescue, and resolved to stem the tide till spring at least.

41

Three weeks brought unexpected relief. Hearing of a vacancy in the family of Mrs. E. Langdon Elwyn, an aged widow, of great wealth and high social station, who resided, with her daughter, on West Penn Square, he ventured to try for the place. She questioned him closely as to his antecedents, qualifications and habits, and then laid down a lengthy code of duties and rules of conduct, from which she never permitted even the slightest departure. The interview was awfully solemn, and, though he had been told of her iron-clad rules and vigorous methods, he found he had formed no correct idea of her severely dignified ways and wonderfully aristocratic formula of domestic government. He answered her multitudinous questions with many misgivings, and hope was lost entirely when he confessed to the truth, that he had had no previous experience at waiting. Strange to say, he was not dismissed, but was asked to bring references. These were brought, and they proved satisfactory. He was engaged at the sum of fourteen dollars per month, and immediately left the hotel to enter upon his new duties. He found the great lady as exacting as she had given herself out, but found also that she was ever ready to appreciate effort on his part to have her rules obeyed and the duties she imposed properly performed. This was an unexpected source of encouragement. It made him anxious to please, and reconciled him to a service which, under less favorable auspices, he could not but have despised. He brought all his prudence to bear on the situation, went through with his labors cautiously and correctly, and soon became her trusted man of all work, keeping the house and grounds in repair, bearing messages, going to the bank, and attending the market, for which purpose a stipulated sum was placed in his hands each month, subject to an accurate account rendered at the end of the time.

As these duties were light, and of a strictly routine order, they did not occupy nearly all his time. The leisure he earned was given to books. As soon as the good lady discovered his taste in this direction, she extended all the encouragement she could. She would select books for him to read from her well-stored library, and, having had large acquaintance with leading public men and families, and enjoyed much travel at home and abroad, she often entertained him for hours by her eloquent disquisitions on men and measures, and her lucid descriptions of scenes and manners in the old world and the new. She willingly honored his request to keep up his connection with the Sunday-school at the Moral Reform Retreat, on Lombard street, a concession he was anxious for, but which he did not expect from one whose code was so unbending. All in all, this was the pleasantest life he had led since he entered the city, and, in a mental and disciplinary point of view, it was by far the most profitable school he had ever attended. He got a larger knowledge of books, new notions of men, public measures, and society in general, and learned many valuable lessons on the nature and necessity of duty, order and economy, from a source so high in wealth and station that their studied existence there was a surprise to him. But, more than all, he learned that the appreciation of energy, industry, care, honor, honesty and sobriety was not, among people of wealth, intelligence and true refinement, limited by race or color, and that these qualities, persistently exercised, would redound to the credit of their possessor and eventuate in his elevation and advancement, no matter whether that possessor were white, black, red, brown or yellow.

The following summer this good old lady went travelling and left the entire charge of the house in his keeping. Such a mark of confidence could not but be flattering, and he felt that the qualities of head and heart he had relied on for promotion were standing him in good stead. After he had been with her a little over a year she broke up housekeeping and went to boarding at the northwest corner of Thirteenth and Walnut streets, in the old Butler mansion, where the Philadelphia Club now has its quarters. She took him with her, and there his duties, modified by the changed situation, were the same as before. In about six months she left the city and went to reside with her daughter, Mrs. Irwin, in New York.

Her departure ended his engagement, and sorry enough he was to part with one who had taken such a kind interest in him, and had contributed so much to his advancement, mentally, socially and morally. His memory of this excellent lady will never fade, and his heart will never fail to be thankful for her favor, confidence and teaching, all of which, so suddenly and unexpectedly interjected into his career, and so directly promotive of his welfare, he cannot but regard as providential.

He was now out in the world again, and his old-time thought of business for himself returned. He had some money saved, and was anxious to test the truth of the adage, "A nimble sixpence is better than a slow dollar." But nothing of a favorable business nature turned up, and, armed with a splendid reference from Mrs. Elwyn, he secured a place at service in the family of William Wurtz, on Walnut street, a retired merchant and an elder in Dr. Barnes' church. Here he had plenty of work, and was not long in securing the confidence of his employer and his family. The same concession as to his Sunday-school was cheerfully made, and many other favors shown. Everything went smoothly till, in the fall of 1847, he heard that a clerk was wanted in the office of the Pennsylvania Anti-Slavery Society, located at 107 North Fifth street.

A MARRIED MAN
AND IN THE ANTI-SLAVERY OFFICE

He made application for the position to Peter Lester, one of the Executive Committee, who sent him to J. Miller McKim, the general agent, corresponding secretary, and gentleman in charge of the office. Mr. McKim received him kindly, and told him he had better write a letter to the Committee, making application for the place, which formality was doubtless suggested in order to get a knowledge of his composition and penmanship. He addressed the committee as follows:

PHILADELPHIA, September 21, 1847
J. M. McKIM, ESQ.,

Dear Sir:—I have duly considered your proposal to me, and I have come to the conclusion of availing myself of the privilege esteeming it no small honor, to be placed in a position where I shall be considered an intelligent being, notwithstanding the salary may be small. Therefore, if you think proper to condescend to confer the favor upon me, I am at your service, sir.

I have viewed the matter in various ways, but have only come to the one conclusion at last, and that is this: if I am not directly rewarded, perhaps it may be the means of more than rewarding me in some future days. I go for liberty and improvement.

Yours respectfully,
WILLIAM STILL

After time had been given the Committee to consider the letter, he called at the office and found that they were inclined to take him, provided the salary suited. On inquiry as to what it was, they said $3.75 per week. It was not an inviting sum, but the field was new; there was fine opportunity to get acquainted with leading anti-slavery people, and perhaps equal opportunity for him to turn his sympathies and energies to the account of his enslaved or escaping brethren, though it was understood that regular Underground Railroad work formed no part of the duties of the place for which he was an applicant. This delicate work was supposed to devolve on older, cooler and abler heads than those found on mere clerical shoulders.

After some little consideration the place was accepted. It required a little consideration, for it must not be thought that he had remained all this time unmoved by the tender passion. On the contrary, he had loved and wooed and won a lady, and, having made her his wife, without any ostentatious ceremony, with not even the accustomed show of gilded card, mountainous cake, pyramidal fruit, ruby wines, or toileted reception, had just set up housekeeping in an humble way in two rooms on Washington street. He had, therefore, to think of more than one, and his acceptance of the clerical place was with the hope that soon the salary might be raised, or that some additional work might be found, by means of which he could eke out a comfortable subsistence for himself and wife.

He found that his immediate duties in the office would consist of attention to its order and cleanliness, distribution of documents through the mails and otherwise, and the mailing of the *Pennsylvania Freeman*, which was published at the office. These duties were not very arduous, and the leisure enjoyed was employed in mental improvement. Mr. McKim was absent a great deal, attending to anti-slavery work, and during his absence the office was quite a propitious place for study. There was no night-work, except on mailing nights. William's first attempt to enlarge his limited income, therefore, took the shape of an attempt to raise and teach a night-school. He got a room up-town, and, gathering a few scholars together, began a pedagogic career. This labor proved too great for the amount of pay. Before the winter was over he gave the project up.

Meanwhile, he grew in knowledge of office duties and affairs, constantly enlarged his ability to be of service

47

to his employers and the cause they represented, and was greatly pleased with every phase of the situation, the pay only excepted. One by one, he became acquainted, even intimate, with the members of the Executive Committee, whom he learned to respect for their hearty kindness and ardent sympathy, and to love for their earnest, unselfish efforts in behalf of his enslaved brethren. Feeling that their names cannot be too firmly fixed in our literature, nor made too familiar by oft repetition, especially among those who must ever be interested readers of whatever appertains to emancipation, we take the liberty of inserting them in this sketch of his life.

Names of the Executive Committee of the Pennsylvania
Anti-Slavery Society.

ROBERT PURVIS, *Pres.*	LUCRETIA MOTT
LINDLEY COATES, *Vice-Pres.*	MISS SARAH PUGH
JAMES MOTT, *Vice-Pres.*	BENJAMIN C. BACON
MISS MARY GREW, *Cor. Sec.*	J. LINDON PENNOCK
HAWORTH WETHERALD, *Rec. Sec.*	ROWLAND JOHNSON
E. M. DAVIS, *Treas.*	SAMUEL T. CHILD

Learning that a janitor was wanted at the Apprentices' Library, southwest corner of Fifth and Arch, and that the services would be performed very early in the morning and in the evenings, before his own office opened and after it closed, he sought and procured the place at a salary of six dollars per month, Benjamin H. Hollingshead being president of the Board. This auxiliary position he held for two years, and until he was able to command larger wages as clerk in the Anti-Slavery Office. All this time his wife carried on dress-making, thus adding something handsome to their income. They lived modestly, but plentifully and enjoyably, and felt that they were working out a mission under auspices for which they should be very grateful.

Soon the anticipated increase in his clerical wages came about. He was given seven dollars a week, which was afterwards still further increased, and it is fair to presume that his employers felt he was worth this to them. At any rate, his duties had grown far beyond those originally prescribed. He had become an earnest, confidential worker in Underground Railroad matters. His house had become known as a safe and convenient station on the line of northward march. He had begun to conduct and carefully note and preserve those examinations of fugitives which, in their printed form, now make his book, the *Underground Railroad Records*. Ofttimes in possession of secret and advance information as to the designs and movements of fugitives, his color enabled him to give aid and perform service which, in the hands of white people, however willing or friendly, could not have been done so delicately, unsuspiciously, or effectively. Thus he wrought in the midst of all that strange, thrilling history, and through all those exciting, perilous times preceding the great rebellion and emancipation. His service with the society covered a period of fourteen years. It was earnest, episodical service, a work of hand, head, and heart, an object of entire enlistment and profound interest then, a source of supreme pride and consolation now.

To illustrate the character of his work by recital of the many incidents of escape and adventure which came under his notice, and with which he, as an humble attaché of the society, was connected, would swell this brief narrative of his life to undue proportions. Besides, this is unnecessary, for the reader will find them all in the *Records* proper. Yet one or two must be mentioned, not only as involving personal history, but as serving to bring out a few points more fully than has heretofore been proper or possible.

The first is the celebrated Colonel John H. Wheeler affair, which serves to illustrate the legal difficulties and personal dangers into which his work led him, as well as all concerned, and in what an imperative way the demand for action often came. It may serve, too, to impress on the mind of the reader the spirit of promptitude which ever characterized his responses to what he deemed his calls of duty. Whenever the message came, day or night, Sunday or Monday, whether in church or about his weekly duties, he never failed to give speedy ear and prompt effort, for he ever felt as one bound with those in bonds.

Colonel Wheeler was United States Minister to Central America. Word came to the office from Bloodgood's Hotel, at the foot of Walnut street, that he was there, accompanied by his slave servant, Jane Johnson, and two children, and that he was about to depart on the outgoing steamer. William ran with all haste to the scene; at the same time Passmore Williamson did the same. On arriving, the colored porters about whispered, "On the boat! On the boat!" Running up on the deck he found them, and told them they were, under the laws of the State, free, and at liberty to go with him. They shrank, in terror of their master, from the proposition. Just then Williamson interfered in her behalf. His statement of the case to Wheeler led to an altercation, in which they clinched and soon were in a scuffle. This gave opportunity for the escape of the slaves. They were taken ashore, rushed into a carriage, driven to the lower part of the city, and at night given shelter at William's house. Wheeler issued warrants for the arrest of Williamson, William Still, and several of the colored porters, the charge being abduction, attempt to incite riot, breach of peace, and so on. Williamson's father was promptly on hand with a writ of habeas corpus and Edward Hopper as attorney, but the son failed to put in an appearance. Judge Kane postponed the case for a day, when Williamson appeared, and, failing to give satisfactory excuse for his absence, was sentenced for contempt of court to indefinite imprisonment, or until he was willing to purge himself of contumacy. This was a very momentous sentence and imprisonment in the annals of the Anti-Slavery Society. It stirred sentiment greatly throughout all the free States. He was visited in confinement by anti-slavery people from all parts, congratulated for the bold stand he had taken, and urged to remain firm, as a test of the rectitude of his position and the cause he represented.

The cases against William and the other colored men came on in due time. The attorneys interested were Charles Gibbons, Charles Gilpin and others. The employees of the railroad and boat swore dead against them. Jane Johnson was brought on the stand under protection, and told a simple, straightforward story, which favored the defendants

51

much. William was acquitted, but the others were convicted and sentenced. Before these trials came on, an article reciting the details of the case, and designed to stir the feeling of the country still deeper, appeared in the New York *Tribune* over William Still's name. This article, which was copied widely and commented on largely, admirably served the purpose for which it was intended. See a full account, taken from the *Underground Railroad Records*, in the appendices of this volume, pages 137 – 56.

In the *Underground Railroad Records* (also reproduced in the appendices, pages 157 – 92), will be found the history of another celebrated case, known as the Christiana affair, a part of which is personal to William Still, if the whole matter does not, in some sense, turn on information which was early imparted to him and upon which he took prompt action. A son of Judge Kane left word at the anti-slavery office that warrants were being prepared for the arrest of the slaves who were hiding in the neighborhood of the Gap and Christiana, Lancaster county, Pennsylvania, and that in a day or two their masters, with the Marshal and a posse, would go up to make the arrests. Mr. McKim said that word must be got to the fugitives at once, and asked William if he could get any one to convey it. He knew one Samuel Williams, who had lived in the neighborhood of Christiana, and being a trusty man, willing to act as messenger, he deputized him to go as bearer of the information on the condition that his expenses should be borne. The slaves were thus put on their guard. How they armed themselves, the reception they gave their masters and the trials which followed, form the narrative found in the *Records* as above indicated. After they were brought to the city William was authorized by the old Abolition Society to visit them in confinement, and to see that all their immediate personal wants were attended to. There was much account made of the poor fellows, who had risked their lives in defence of their liberty, and whose action led to such vital tests of laws and constitutions. Among the other evidences of appreciation shown them by distinguished citizens was a magnificent Christmas dinner served to them by Thomas L. (afterwards General) Kane. William's mission to the prisoners was made easy by the kindness of the then U. S. Marshal, Mr. Anthony E. Roberts, of Lancaster county, Pennsylvania, who, without any compromise of his official dignity or duty, placed at his disposal passes to the jail in sufficient numbers to admit all who wished to sympathize with and console them.

Mention must also be made here of a few hitherto unpublished facts connected with, and growing out of, the John Brown capture of Harper's Ferry. October 17th, 1859, six months before the old hero and his brave band struck their blow at the Ferry, the plans were submitted to William Still by Frederick Douglass, who seemed to be fully up in all the secrets of the campaign, and who was expected to play a leading part in it. He, William, could not see that it was feasible, regarded it as a venture sure to end in disaster, and as an attempt involving more of desperation than valor, more of precipitation than prudence. Indeed, he had not persuaded himself that open hostilities could, or would, begin in the manner proposed to him until he

53

was startled by news of their occurrence, on the morning of the outbreak.

The country was ablaze with excitement North and South. The proslavery sentiment was never so aggressive, inquisitorial, and bloodthirsty. It threatened death to abolitionism, and arrests were frequent in Massachusetts and throughout the Northern States. No anti-slavery man bold enough to speak his thoughts, or brave enough to exert himself in behalf of his principles was, for a moment, safe from arrest and imprisonment, at least; what more he did not know. Of course William, with all the rest in Philadelphia, felt that his hour might arrive at any time, and that prudence demanded that nothing to attract attention to himself should be done, till the storm had spent its fury.

Two days before the attack on the Ferry a suspicious letter came to the office addressed to Captain Watkins. It was not interfered with till the battle began. Then, in fear of its contents, it was put where no man could find it. More startling still, in the mass of documents and inculpatory letters captured from Captain John Henry Kagi—most of which the newspapers greedily published—was a memorandum to this effect, "Wrote William Still Wednesday." This was not very comfortable information to get abroad. It might prove a rod which would bring the lightning directly to his door. He turned his attention to packing up the Underground Railroad Records, and getting all evidence of that kind out of the way.

A few days of terror and suspense passed. Just as the thought was dawning that perhaps the worst was over there arrived at his house, late one afternoon, a tired, foot-sore, famished, powder-begrimed fugitive, whose waist was encircled with a belt filled with revolvers. It was Lieutenant Francis J. Merriem, grandson of the great Boston abolitionist and philanthropist, Francis Jackson, and one of John Brown's leading officers. Here was a plight more serious than ever, a danger not before contemplated. If the lieutenant were pursued, there would be battle within the very walls of his house, and the life of no inmate would be spared. At any rate the safety of all concerned demanded that so conspicuous a fugitive should not spend much time at any one retreat. In the evening William succeeded in getting him into the hands of Dr. I. Newlin Pierce (a true and tried abolitionist). He was provided with money by William, and started for Canada, his desire being to avoid Boston, where he had wealthy relatives and warm friends.

This embarrassing episode over, another followed in quick succession. All unheralded, Captain Osborne Anderson, who had been in the hottest of the battle at the Ferry, came to his house for protection. A big reward had been offered for his arrest, with all other participants, by Governor Wise, of Virginia. He was literally in rags—but these were a disguise. In his belt were two revolvers. He had no money. The reward would bring the officers of the law beyond a doubt, and that speedily. The harborer would suffer with the harbored. Prompt action was necessary. The secret of his presence was entrusted to J. Miller McKim and Passmore Williamson, outside of his family, only. One day of rest was given, then, furnished with a new suit and tickets for Canada, he too passed safely over the border via the Underground Railroad.

Meanwhile preparations were going on for the trial of John Brown at Charlestown. In the midst of the agitation attending these steps, his wife, Mary A. Brown, came to William's house on her way to visit her husband in his cell. She was made comfortable as possible under the circumstances, and was visited by many friends, who united to dissuade her from her proposed trip, as excitement was running too high, and she would be likely to be disappointed in her aim. She finally yielded to their advice, and remained in the city for a couple of weeks, spending a week with Mr. McKim and a few days with Thomas Dorsey.

During the period between Brown's trial and execution, and while the officers of the law and slave-holders were eagerly seeking for everyone connected with him and his expedition, three other persons came under William's roof who had been identified with the expedition, who were under suspicion for their complicity, and whose secret object was to test sentiment as to the practicability of an attempt to raid the jail and rescue the condemned man. Their presence made his home situation as delicate and dangerous as if they had been fugitives directly from the scene of battle, for, while they all came and went safely, they were all fully armed and resolved to die rather than submit to arrest and ignominious death on the scaffold. Their names were John Brown, Jr., son of the condemned, James Redpath, journalist, and afterwards author of *The Old Hero, John Brown*, and another whose name has not been preserved. Thus William figured as an actor in those thrilling, dangerous and swiftly-changing scenes. How different the result might have been for all concerned had he proved less cool of head, less prompt of action, less brave of heart, or had he failed, through lack of shrewdness, to take in and command each situation as it projected itself suddenly on his attention and into his life! Yea, and how differently it all might have been had he not been blessed with a wife, Letitia, who possessed like intuitions, who was equally ardent in the cause, and always judicious and patient when emergency crossed her threshold. When, as during the last decade of slavery, arrivals of fugitives were of almost daily occurrence, and perhaps ninety-five per cent of those fleeing to Canada by way of Philadelphia found needed rest and food under his humble roof, it is very evident that the position of his wife was one of constant care and anxiety, that her domestic duties were thereby rendered much more laborious, and that the sudden comings of unheralded fugitives must have greatly disturbed the order and serenity of her household. Yet amid every ordeal, whether to open the door and receive the fugitive by day or night; whether to feed them at any hour; whether to provide temporary beds for more than could otherwise be accommodated; whether to wash and mend dirty and tattered garments—tasks which often occupied her long after midnight; whether to nurse sick mothers and helpless children, or dress wounds received in flight; whether to secrete them quickly or hide them away suddenly when danger impended; whether in one or all of these, she was ever ready and willing to do herself or help her husband do, and that without murmur or plaint. Amid the perils which constantly surrounded her she never showed a fear. Every sacrifice she was called upon to make was cheerfully met, and every secret she became the possessor of was sacredly kept. Ever her husband's counterpart in interest and enthusiasm, ever his equal in fortitude, she added to the help she always gave those womanly qualities of patience, tenderness, suavity and constancy, which served then, as they did of old, and ever will, to make her ministrations angelic.

After the Wheeler affair above mentioned, and in the year 1855, William concluded that a visit to Canada, to look into the condition of the fugitives domiciled there, and to see how they could be further aided, would prove mutually profitable. He got leave of absence and prepared himself for an extended trip by securing letters of introduction and recommendation from prominent members of the Society. These letters he has preserved with great care. Two or three are introduced here to show the spirit which pervaded the writers, and the esteem in which he was held by his employers. The first is over the signatures of the beloved Lucretia Mott and her faithful husband.

PHILADELPHIA, 9th Month, 5th, 1855
*To the Lovers of Liberty and Friends of Humanity
in Canada*:

Our highly-esteemed and well-beloved friend, William Still, of this city, being about to visit Canada to inspect the condition of the colored people, many of whom are largely indebted to him for their deliverance from the bonds of slavery, we commend him to the kind regard of all he may meet as a man worthy of honor.

JAMES MOTT,
LUCRETIA MOTT

This from Professor Charles D. Cleveland, one of the foremost abolitionists of the country:

PHILADELPHIA, September 8, 1855
To the Friends of Freedom in Canada:
My friend, William Still, of this city, being about to visit Canada, wishes from me a general letter of introduction. This I give with very great pleasure, and commend him most cordially to every one as a most intelligent, consistent and devoted friend of the oppressed of his race. Indeed, where we are both equally well known, I should be complimented quite as much with a testimony of faithfulness to freedom from him as he from me; and wherever he may go I trust that all who love freedom and hate slavery will do what they can to aid him in his benevolent mission. Praying that God's blessing may attend him in his labor of love, and that he may return in safety, I am his sincere friend,

CHARLES D. CLEVELAND

And this from his ever-faithful friend and adviser, J. Miller McKim:

ANTI-SLAVERY OFFICE,
PHILADELPHIA, September 10, 1855
To Thomas Henning, Esq.,

Dear Sir: The bearer of this is William Still, my assistant in this office and my personal friend; allow me to introduce him to you as one worthy of your regard.

Mr. Still is the secretary and agent of the Philadelphia Vigilance Committee, and goes to Canada on a tour of observation connected with the duties of his office.

I commend him to your kind offices, and trust that, for the sake of the cause in which we have a common interest, you will do what you can to promote the object of his mission.

> Yours very truly,
> J. M. McKim,
> *Cor. Sec. of the Pa. A. S. Society*

Starting on his visit, he stopped for a time at all the places where the fugitives were colonized, or which were centres of information for those who made their homes in the country. Among these places were Toronto, St. Catherines, Hamilton, Ontario, Kingston, Chatham, Buxton, etc. For a long time prior to his trip he had been a constant correspondent of the *Provincial Freeman*, published at Chatham, by Miss Mary Ann Shadd, a colored woman of great ability, and one heartily devoted to the emancipation and elevation of her race. He found the fugitives in good spirits, well cared for, and evincing a disposition to care for themselves by industry and frugality. Though new to freedom, they were not disposed to abuse it. They were eager for news, and responsive to the advice and teachings of those who had helped them to a changed estate, and were anxious to see them prosper in it. Altogether his trip was one of great pleasure and profit to himself, and he returned home indulging the hope that, mayhap, his mission was not void of similar results for those whom he went out to see. One curiosity of it will bear mention. Those whom he visited had heard much more of him in advance than he suspected, and it was oftentimes quite comical to see their expression of face and hear their remarks when they found he was not the hoary-headed, wrinkled-visaged and bowed old patriarch their fancies had pictured him to be. William was accompanied on this trip by his brother, Dr. James Still, of New Jersey.

The pro-slavery people were very emphatic in their opinion and argument that a slave would never prove himself of any account once he was out of bondage. In order to controvert this, William, after what he had seen in Canada, prepared an article which appeared in the *North American* of February 1, 1860, and which is here reproduced in brief.

As will be seen, it quotes a paragraph from the *Public Ledger* of January 21, 1860, which was but one of many which had been going the rounds of the anti-slavery press.

"'THE COLORED POPULATION IN CANADA—The Canadians are beginning to experience the evil of the encouragement which they have given to fugitive slaves escaping from the United States. In some districts they outnumber the white population, and of course wish to rule by the power of numbers. Collisions are becoming common between them and the white population, and the laws are obstructed by riot and other outrages. The town of Chatham, on Monday last, was in a state of excitement owing to the colored people taking possession of the public school-houses and refusing to let the white teacher and children into the schools. They had hitherto had schools of their own, but now insisted that the schools shall be opened in common to whites and blacks. The mayor and authorities had to quiet the hubbub by consenting to take the matter into consideration. The feeling of the people is, however, so great that there is every prospect of a riot if the mayor consents to the demand. In Sandwich similar disturbances from the same demand occurred. The hate of races has begun in Canada, and it will be quite as "irrepressible" as the contest between slavery and anti-slavery.'

"Although this article from the *Ledger* is very brief, it is, nevertheless, very damaging, and misrepresents entirely the facts of the case relative to the colored people in Canada, and that to a degree that could not possibly be corrected by the simple paragraph alluded to on the subject. It is obvious, of course, that the *Ledger* founded its charges on reports from the journals alluded to above. Hence, I wish to present in reply such facts as shall not be subject to truthful gainsay— such facts as I witnessed with my own eyes while in Canada on a visit of observation and examination into the condition of the colored people; also such facts as I have had opportunity of gathering from various other sources for a long time. First, with regard to Chatham. In this town the entire population is from seven to eight thousand, the colored inhabitants *not exceeding fifteen hundred*. This does not look as though 'they outnumbered the white population.' Nevertheless, it is well known from one end of Canada to the other that the colored people are nowhere so thickly settled in any town or district as at Chatham. Nowhere in Canada do they approximate in numbers so near the whites as there, and although they have the right, and exercise the franchise freely in common with all other citizens, they have never attempted to organize a colored party; they have always been loyal, voting with the regular '*Reform party*' or the '*Conservative party*' (the only parties in Canada), same as all other citizens vote.

"The assertion, therefore, that they 'wish to rule by the power of numbers,' or that 'collisions are becoming common,' or that the 'laws are obstructed by riot and other outrages,' certainly is sustained by no more truth than were the allegations that the 'Negroes had taken possession of the schools,' etc.

"The truth is, the colored people of Chatham, as a general thing, are industrious, peaceable, and prosperous. They have four churches, three schools, one or two fire companies, one company of soldiers. In mechanical trades they may be found as masons, plasterers, blacksmiths, cabinet-makers, carpenters, shoemakers, one watchmaker, and one gunsmith, two or three wheelwrights and carriage-makers, and last, though not least, they have one printing-press. In the city market a large proportion of the butchers, as well as the farmers with produce cultivated on their own lands, are colored men. In office at this time there is but one colored man—he is a constable.

"The testimony of Dr. J. Wilson Moore and his lady (Rachel Barker Moore), of this city, is apropos:

"They visited Canada in July and August, 1858, expressly with the view of ascertaining the true condition of the colored people for themselves. A few brief extracts from their letters will show what they thought of the condition of the colored people:

"'We arrived at Chatham, C. W., on the second of the eighth month, 1858, whilst the colored people were celebrating the abolition of slavery in the British West Indies. We saw them returning from their various places of meeting, where we were informed many excellent speeches were delivered, both by white and colored people. Their orderly deportment would have done honor to any class of citizens—not a single inebriate was discovered amongst them.

63

"'We attended a fair in the evening, gotten up by the females to aid in building a meeting-house, which was conducted with perfect order and decorum.

"'On the 3d we made a number of calls on the colored inhabitants of Chatham, and found them comfortable and happy.'

"Of London they say:

"'On our arrival at New London we found a large number residing in that city. My wife, accompanied by two friends, visited several of the families in order to ascertain for herself their real condition. (Being unwell, I was unable to accompany her.) All she saw or heard was favorable to their moral and intellectual condition; their houses possessed an air of neatness and comfort, and some have accumulated considerable substance.'

"Of the Wilberforce settlement they speak thus:

"'We visited nearly all the families in their own houses, most of them having escaped from bondage. We had much conversation with them relative to their early settlement, their present condition and standing in society, and were informed that at first they had to endure deprivations and hardships, but perseverance, industry, and economy had enabled them to overcome all opposition, and little by little to clear the forest and establish themselves in peace and plenty. Their log-cabins are giving place to brick and frame houses, their farming operations are prosperous, and their condition in life is assuming quite a comfortable aspect. Their standing is fair, and the laws of the land know no distinction. They sit on juries with their white neighbors, are school-directors and road-commissioners, and are respected as much as their intelligence and virtue entitle them to be.

"'Such is the result of the labor and toil of the persevering pioneer, who, having to endure many privations in the morning of life, may be blessed with plenty, with their children around them growing up into wealth and respectability, with all the advantages of receiving a good education to fit them for the business of life. Far better would it be for those who congregate in towns and cities to emigrate as they have done,' etc.

"Unquestionably the statements made by Dr. Moore and his wife were very carefully made and are correct.

"To say that there are not those amongst the colored people in Canada, as every place, who are very poor (many of them have had but precious little chance to be rich), who will commit crime, who indulge in habits of indolence and intemperance (the laws where they may have been raised probably prohibited education), would be far from the truth. Nevertheless, may not the same be said of white people, even where they have had the best chances in every particular?

"Again, if the colored citizens of Canada were the 'lawless, lazy wretches' that they are represented to be by the *Detroit Free Press*, etc., would not the Canadian Parliament, the intelligent press, the rigidly impartial laws of the land find a way of enlightening the public in relation to this class of settlers, and adopt measures to prohibit their emigration? It cannot be said that sympathy for the negro prevents them from acting, for it is an undeniable fact that the white Canadians manifest no particular sympathy for the negro. They neither encourage his coming, nor offer objections against it. True, Mr. Larwell, an ex-member of Parliament, a rabid negro-hater, but without influence, while in Parliament offered from time to time bills, and made speeches against colored people coming to Canada, but his bills invariably fell dead, without receiving a single second. It is also true that Colonel Prince, now a member of Parliament, two years ago, in Parliament and in the press, heaped upon the colored settlers no small amount of censure and odium (although actually elected by colored votes), yet his charges were promptly met and refuted, both in Parliament and by the leading press of Canada, and it had just no more effect than would be produced by a violent Native American speech in Congress or the press of this country against foreigners and foreign emigration. Indeed, it is said on good authority that even Colonel Prince has since taken back his wholesale charges against the negro. I have confined myself to a simple statement of facts, Mr. Editor, and if you will publish them you will greatly oblige."

Philadelphia, January 30th, 1860
Yours respectfully,
WILLIAM STILL

The operations of the Underground Railroad were particularly active from 1855 to 1859. In 1857 William prepared an extended article, covering the workings of the road for a single month of that year. During that month as many as sixty fugitives, old and young, male and female, had been sent northward on freedom's journey. After mature thought, he concluded that its publication would eventuate in great good to the cause. So an understanding was had with Mr. Greeley that the author's name should be kept "confidential," with no squinting toward Philadelphia, and the article appeared in the *Tribune* dated from Niagara Falls, and signed V. C.—Vigilance Committee. It contained a brief account of each passenger, the owners, the names of the places where held in bondage, the characters of the different masters, the motives which prompted flight, the advertisements and heavy rewards offered for recovery. There was no attempt made to varnish or enlarge upon the simple narratives of these fugitives. As was anticipated, the article created no little stir in and out of Underground Railroad circles, especially in Maryland and Virginia, whence most of the escapes were made.

William's connection with the anti-slavery office had now extended over a period of fourteen years. The year 1860 had been reached and the country was on the verge of that great outbreak, that final clash of arms, which resulted in emancipation and, let it be hoped, a stronger union of States. At this juncture it became expedient for him to cease his connection with the office, not that slavery was extinct, nor that the work of the Underground Railroad had ended, but owing to stringency in money matters the office found retrenchment necessary. In one sense he was quite reconciled to his severance, for the office would still retain as its general agent and corresponding secretary, Mr. J. Miller McKim, to whom the cause was more largely indebted for its organized and positive efficiency than to any other man in Pennsylvania. And it would still retain another whose name cannot be too well-known to the colored race, nor held in too high esteem. We allude to Mr. Charles Wise who, some ten years prior to the overthrow of slavery, became treasurer of the Underground Railroad corporation, and remained so till the end came. He was head of the mercantile house of Wise, Pusey & Wise, at northeast corner of Fifth and Market streets. Devoted to his business, he was no less interested in that of the underground railroad. Indeed he was almost a daily visitor at the anti-slavery office for purposes of information, and his services were never required at the regular depot that he did not respond, sometimes to the extent of four and five times a week, when travel was lively. He met all comers with a cordial greeting and extended the right hand of fellowship so warmly and naturally as to win their immediate confidence. Not infrequently he would spend two or three hours talking with them and listening to their thrilling narratives. Sometimes he would prolong his interviews far into the night, and make William very anxious for his departure in order that he might have a chance to jot down their sad histories before train time. No matter how many arrivals there were—two, three, five, or a dozen—Charles Wise wanted to hear from all, had ever a good word for all, and never seemed so much delighted as when the business of the road was brisk.

In another sense William's separation from the office seemed to him a regretful step, in that it would sever business relations with the Executive Committee and their host of coadjutors, and break in upon an official relationship which had always been of the pleasantest and most assuring kind. Yet, that these brave spirits, true friends, and wise counsellors, were now acting for his own good and that of the cause in obeying economic dictates, he never doubted.

He therefore prepared his letter of resignation, in which he expressed his very warm regard for the committee, and his recognition of the necessity which compelled regretful severance of an official connection which he should ever look back to with pride, and would ever find a source of happy memories.

The committee responded through their secretary, Mr. McKim, as follows:

Philadelphia, June 1,1861
To WILLIAM STILL:

Dear Friend:—I am directed by the Executive Committee to acknowledge the receipt of your letter of resignation and to express to you the regret they feel at the necessity which compels them without demur to accept it. The relations which have existed between them and you for so many years have been altogether satisfactory, and they most cordially reciprocate all the kind feelings in this regard which you are pleased to express in your letter. They desire me to testify to you their lively appreciation of the integrity, ability and uniform courtesy which have ever characterized you in the discharge of your duties, and to express the hope and belief that these qualities—which have made you so acceptable in their service—will insure you all reasonable success in the new line of business which it is understood you are hereafter to pursue.

Trusting that, though not bound together by any official tie, we may always continue united as coadjutors in the common cause, I am, on behalf of the committee,

Yours most truly,
J. M. McKIM,
Cor. Sec. of Pa. A. S. Society

Here ended that portion of his life which, more than any previous part, had been eventful and full of opportunities to learn the world and serve a cause as dear to him as life. It is easy for the reader to form an opinion of how he had enlarged his powers for usefulness, how profited by experiences, how prepared himself for the undertakings, one of his active temperament and laudable ambitions would find in the near future. Let it never be forgotten that this part of his career was, as every former one had been, a full vindication of his life's doctrine that color is not a barrier to success, if the laws of success are properly understood and practiced.

BECOMES AN AUTHOR

It may seem strange that one whose tastes inclined him so much to business as Mr. Still's, should become an author. Ordinarily, literary and business tastes and aspirations do not meet in the same person. But Mr. Still had ever been a great reader of newspapers, magazines and books. He had often keenly reflected on the fact that in the fields of literature through which he delighted to roam in quest of something new and striking in art, science, politics or religion, the pen of those with whom he bore race relations seldom appeared. The chasm which slavery had made between white and black was widest in the fields of literature. This not only deepened his detestation of the accursed institution, but begat in him a profound sympathy for those of his race who were struggling to narrow or bridge this chasm by becoming editors or authors. From his younger days, even before he was out of his teens, no attempt of a colored man or woman to publish a paper, write a book, or push a literary enterprise that came to his notice, failed to receive his appreciation and, nearly always, his material aid. He was wont to correspond for such papers, secure subscriptions, and help introduce books without other compensation than the delight which success afforded, and the pride which everything that enured to the credit of his race engendered.

As an instance of his interest in this direction, when Dr. William Wells Brown, the intrepid author and able advocate of freedom and temperance, published his book, called *The Black Man*, he at once ordered and paid cash for one hundred copies. So, when Mrs. F. E. W. Harper (then Miss Watkins) came to Philadelphia, thirty years ago, a stranger and without letters of introduction to any influential person, bearing a little book written in verse and prose, which showed great powers of thought and a beautiful ordering of mind, he strove to secure for her a literary recognition, in a private way, among his anti-slavery friends. When they doubted the originality of her writings, or regarded them as exceeding her ability, he, knowing that she had oratorical gifts, got her to appear in the Assembly Building before an audience of abolitionists. Her effort on this occasion left no room to doubt her wonderful powers. Since then, where has she not entranced multitudes by her eloquence and moved myriads to tears by her inimitable pathos? Her little books have been published and sold by the tens of thousands, and she is to-day the best known colored poetess and lady speaker on this continent.

Nor was his interest in this direction confined only to those literary enterprises which worked directly to the advantage of his race. For instance—and this is but one of many—when the country was yet rocking amid the billows stirred by rebellion, and when the problems which concerned the rescued millions were even mightier than those which led to their rescue, it was thought by able men who had been instrumental in bringing about abolition that the time was ripe for a paper of commanding ability, strong character, fairness and faithfulness to North, South, East and West, and independence enough for impartial review of politics, science, literature, art, etc. To establish such a paper, $100,000 was deemed requisite. This was subscribed on regular stock principles, with Mr. McKim taking a leading part in forwarding the project. Of this stock, Mr. Still took $1,000 worth. The paper appeared as *The Nation*.

These facts show his appreciation of authorship, and his desire to encourage literary effort among his people for their benefit directly and indirectly. While they foreshadow for him an ability to tread the same paths, or indicate a spirit not averse to entering on them, his own work of authorship was not a mapped and studied thing. It was rather a proper thing at a proper time; a natural outcrop of conditions which he was prepared to take advantage of, but which he never expected to see with his own eyes. As to his authorship it may be said, "There is a divinity which shapes our ends, rough-hew them how we will." In pursuance of what he thought a duty in connection with the anti-slavery office, but which many thought to be inconsequential and all impolitic, if not positively dangerous, he unsuspectingly laid the groundwork of a book whose printing and publication emancipation rendered opportune, and which has thus far enjoyed the distinction of being the only volume of the kind made up of records kept from day to day, and minute notations of what actually fell from the lips of those in whose interest the anti-slavery society was founded and the Underground Railroad conducted.

As has been seen, it was no part of the duty of a clerk in the anti-slavery office to attend directly to Underground Railroad affairs. Mr. Still's identity with this important service was in the nature of a growth, though, of course, in the direction of his sympathies and desires, and accelerated by fitness shown for the work. He had hardly become a recognized part of the intricate machinery of the railroad before his attention was attracted to the necessity of records which should comprise and preserve the narratives of the fugitives who sought the protection of the office and the facilities for further flight it provided. He agreed with all interested that the making of such records was of doubtful propriety, and that their existence would be a constant menace to the society as an organization as well as to the individual members thereof. Yet he had promptings for the undertaking which, on account of his color and lineage, lay deeper than questions of expediency, and seemed to warrant such a risk as he knew it would impose.

His motives are best illustrated by the recital of an occurrence, directly in the line of his duty as an attaché of the anti-slavery office, which has all the strange force and thrill of drama, and of which he became an unsuspecting part. This occurrence he has so fully and graphically told in a chapter of unpublished reminiscences, under the head of "Peter Still, the Kidnapped and Ransomed," that we reproduce it here in his own language.*

On one summer day in 1850, as I was busily engaged in mailing the weekly issue of the *Pennsylvania Freeman*, two colored men entered the office. One of them was a resident of Philadelphia and well known to me; the other I had never seen. My acquaintance introduced the stranger as coming from the South, and with the added remark, "He will tell his own story." I paused, and the stranger began in a very deliberate manner, saying, "I am from Alabama. I have come in search of my people. I and my little brother were kidnapped about forty years ago, and I thought by coming to Philadelphia and having notices written and read in the colored churches, old people would remember about it and I could find my mother and people."

After going on with his story for a few minutes in this way, I became fully satisfied that, if his history were as he had given it thus far, I could save valuable time by asking a few questions. I therefore asked, "Where were you kidnapped from?"

A. "I don't know."

Q. "Don't you know the name of the place?"

A. "No."

Q. "Don't you know the name of any town, river, neighborhood or State?"

A. "No."

Q. "What was your name?"

A. "Peter."

---

* See the Appendices, 133 - 36, where more of this story is reproduced from the *Underground Rail Road Records* (1886 edition).

Q. "What was your little brother's name?"

A. "Levin."

Q. "What were the names of your mother and father?"

A. "Mother's name was Sidney, and father's name was Levin."

Q. "Do you remember the name of any other person?"

A. "I know the name of one white man." (Here he named him.)

By this time I was simply thunderstruck, so to speak. I had to summon all my powers of control in the presence of the stranger, so fully was I convinced by this time that he was one of my long-lost brothers. I scarcely knew what to do for a little time, but by and by I dismissed the pilot, saying I would look further into the case after I got done with my mailing, and would take care of the stranger over-night. This was satisfactory to the pilot, but hardly so to the stranger, till he was advised by his friend that it would be all right.

Before intimating to my brother the discovery I had made, I allowed a full hour to pass, meanwhile plying him with a thousand questions touching his entire life. Then, seating myself by his side, I said: "I think I can tell you all about your kinfolk—mother, father, etc.," and went on to say, "You are an own brother of mine."

As anxious as he had been all his life to find his lost parents and relatives, this news was at the moment too good for him to fully credit. He was as one dumbfounded. I went on to assure him of the truth of all I had said by narrating our family history in detail, and dwelling particularly on mother's escapes, and how in her second attempt she was compelled to leave her two little boys, Levin and Peter, behind, in the care of their grandmother.

Having explained the matter to Peter thus fully, his doubts vanished, and he went home with me. His two sisters living in Philadelphia, who were acquainted with all the secrets of the family history, were soon called in, and became joyful witnesses of the marvelous restoration. Outside of myself and my sisters, I felt sure he might have inquired the city over without having obtained the slightest clue to his lost relations.

The next day he was taken to his mother's home in New Jersey and fully recognized by her, not a shadow of doubt appearing as to his identity, for he was her very image.

Allow me to remark just here that it was this heart-rending history connected with my own family that first prompted me to undertake to keep records of the Underground Railroad. Thousands of escapes, harrowing separations, dreadful longings, dark gropings after lost parents, brothers, sisters, and identities, seemed ever to be pressing on my mind. While I knew the danger of keeping strict records, and while I did not then dream that in my day slavery would be blotted out, or that the time would come when I could publish these records, it used to afford me great satisfaction to take them down fresh from the lips of fugitives on the way to freedom, and to preserve them as they had given them. But, thank God! The end of slavery came ere we looked for it, and the records are no longer preserved in secret, nor is their presence a source of danger.

The motives for making and preserving these records must now be clear. It is equally clear that he never expected they would see the light, for as long as slavery existed, their publication, or even discovery, would have resulted in disaster, and the end of slavery was not looked for in his day. The uses he expected them to subserve were of a strictly private nature. The information contained therein he hoped to be able to turn, without other recompense than the satisfaction it afforded, to the account of his fugitive brethren, cut off from knowledge of parents, friends, and even themselves, and always anxious for any clue that might lead to the restoration of lost identities, and the reunion of severed relationships. This will account for the minute descriptions of size, height, shade of complexion, cast of features, age, and striking peculiarities of many of the characters met with in the *Records*.

As one can well imagine, the records he had thus accumulated had swelled to voluminous proportions, which were further augmented by hundreds of preserved letters relating to Underground Railroad affairs. The excitement incident to active war was now on, and soon the bloody drama was to open by the assault on Sumter. Remembering how on two or three occasions prior to this, the greatest precaution had to be taken to keep them where they would not endanger the life of their possessor and all concerned, he now concluded that, amid the greater uncertainty of arms, there was no place about his premises sufficiently safe as a depository. Looking about, he struck on the loft of a Lebanon Cemetery building as a spot likely to insure their safety. Thence they were taken, and, in the custody of Jacob C. White, Sr., one of the most active and reliable members of the Vigilance Committee, were safely stowed away in the very midst of the region of the dead and the land of forgetfulness, where they remained till after war's grim visage was wrapped in the smiles of peace. This assumption of responsibility for them was quite a concession on the part of Mr. White, who had some time before made the remark that, in the event of a disastrous outbreak, "If all his books, papers, and letters were exhumed any day, not even to the extent of a scratch of a pin could anything be found to connect him with the escape of slaves."

All danger passed, Mr. Still turned his attention to his papers, and now he was anxious lest, in escaping capture at human hands, they had fallen a prey to rats and mice, whose proclivity for using papers as bedding is well known. He was further anxious to rescue them because emancipation had not only removed the necessity for secrecy respecting their existence, but had made it possible for him to use them as a history of the perilous times preceding actual war, and of the methods employed by the friends of freedom in behalf of the slave race. He began to feel that this would at least be most curious history for every eye, and that it might prove invaluable to the freedmen of the South as showing the nature of the struggles which were preliminary to actual emancipation, and how their cause had been one which involved the brightest intellect, profoundest sympathy, and most active philanthropy of the civilization in which they were at last, by God's will, invited and permitted to participate.

Yet he was in no hurry to rush into authorship. He knew very well that no similar records were in existence.

Thomas Garrett had been asked by publishers to furnish data appertaining to Underground Railroad matters, but had said he had not kept even so much as "the scratch of a pen." The same was true of Levi Coffin of Cincinnati. He therefore feared no competition in his proposed line. Besides, time, which is the great mellower of feelings, seemed to point to a period in her future as more opportune than the then present, with its waves still lashing the shore after the storm.

These thoughts respecting the records received encouragement from a source so high and so worthy of respect, that propriety about their publication was made to take almost the form of duty. The Pennsylvania Anti-Slavery Society held its closing meeting in May 1871. One of its resolutions, unanimously passed, read as follows:

> WHEREAS, the position of William in the Vigilance Committee connected with the 'Underground Railroad' as its corresponding secretary and chairman of its active sub-committee gave him peculiar facilities for collecting interesting facts pertaining to this branch of the Anti-Slavery service, therefore,
>
> *Resolved*, that the Pennsylvania Anti-Slavery Society request him to compile and publish his personal reminiscences and experiences relating to the 'Underground Railroad.'

In that very year (1871), there was a seven-month strike among the coal miners of Pennsylvania. This made the retail coal trade, in which Mr. Still was then engaged, extremely dull, but it afforded him the leisure which he felt he ought to be able to command before engaging in active work upon the records. Taking advantage of it, and pushing their preparation bravely on, he reached a point where their appearance in book form was to be considered. How was he to arrive at any definite idea of style of type, cost of electrotyping, paper, printing, binding, etc.? Going to his library, he selected a volume which, as to its size, kind of type, quality of paper, and general make-up met his ideal of what his book of *Records* should be. With this as a guide, he went to several first-class electrotypers and printers and asked for estimates. He was not long in closing a satisfactory agreement with a competent man to electrotype his work and print one thousand copies. As to the engravings, he consulted with his old friend, Colonel T. Elwood Zell, publisher of the *Encyclopaedia*, who informed him that he could command, at a reasonable rate, the services of a part of his corps of engravers, as the work on his *Universal Maps* was about completed.

All this was quite satisfactory headway, considering the fact that the seas he was sailing were practically unknown to him. But now came the awful fix into which nearly all authors get themselves, namely, the preparation of copy under the call of the printer. He agreed to furnish the manuscript for four pages of the printed book per day, and the printer agreed to place the same in type. Therefore, yielding to none of the demands of other business or pleasure, he plied his pen from five in the morning till eleven at night. With all this assiduity he must have fallen far short of his part of the contract but for the kindness of Dr. W. H. Furness, so widely known for his sympathy with the slave, and his large-hearted aid in making sure the fugitive's passport to freedom. He volunteered to read the proof, and thus help to facilitate the publication of the work. This signal proof of interest in his undertaking by one so learned and so weighted with other and higher cares was a matter of great moment to Mr. Still. It was not only aid direct, but an endorsement of his undertaking which would prove invaluable. Daily the proofs were carried to his country residence, and daily returned. When the doctor went off on a journey, the son, Horace H. Furness, who has since won world-wide reputation in the path of letters, took up the labor of proof-reading and carried it on with all the father's care and assiduity. The voluntary aid thus afforded by these estimable friends made Mr. Still's debt of obligation so great as to place requital far beyond his reach, save in so far as the highest appreciation and warmest thanks may serve to show the spirit of the beneficiary.

Long before the last pages were in type, word of its prospective existence reached the ears of a number of publishers, and at least six or eight were anxious to contract for its publication. There was but one answer for all and that was, no disposition of it to any one till it was complete, as until then, no one could fairly judge of its merits. The year 1872 saw its completion, and the *Underground Railroad Records*, as a large octavo volume of 800 pages, appeared, under the copyright of its author, William Still. At the close of these literary labors, he made a visit to Washington and other places in the border states of the South, to look into the condition of the freedmen, and especially to see what was being done in the way of providing school facilities for them. He went, bearing letters of introduction from many of his most influential and best known friends, one of which, as a sample of the whole, may be given here.

To A. E. Newton, Esq., 207 I Street, Washington:

My Dear Sir:—Allow me to introduce to you my particular friend William Still, Esq., of Philadelphia. He visits Washington and other southern cities on a tour of observation. He is much interested in freedmen's schools and in all matters that appertain to impartial liberty. Please aid him in seeing what is desirable to see in your city and its neighborhood. Any attention shown him I will regard as a favor to myself. Mr. Still is one of the most enlightened and liberal friends of freedom in this country. You will find him in all respects a gentleman.

Truly yours,
J. M. McKim

He took along with him advanced sheets of his book and submitted them to his friends at the Capitol. All spoke approvingly of his efforts, and many gave him encouraging letters. Chief-Justice Chase wrote him as follows:

Washington, March 1, 1872

Dear Sir:—Your book will certainly be an extremely interesting one. No one probably has had equal opportunities with yourself of listening to the narratives of fugitive slaves. No one will repeat them more truthfully, and no stories can be more fraught with interest than theirs. Let us rejoice that, in our country, such narratives can never be heard again.

Yours truly,
P. CHASE

MR. WILLIAM STILL

That the handwriting of some of the illustrious friends of freedom and of the colored race, who approved of his work and honored him by their favorable mention of it, may be seen and studied, he has gone to the expense of presenting lithographic *fac similes* of the letters he received from three of them. The first is from Hon. Charles Sumner, whose great name is held in reverence by the colored race and the friends of free institutions throughout the civilized world. His letter is the handwriting of the recognized intellectual champion of freedom. Whenever, in the halls of national legislation, the cause of the colored man required an advocate, his voice was first and most potential. When the time came to remodel laws and constitutions so as to make them applicable to a nation of freemen only, his genius was prolific of wise and practical measures, and his mind fruitful of bold, unanswerable arguments in their behalf. Of the few anti-slavery statesmen who excelled him in sagacity, none equaled him in learning. Some were more fiery advocates of freedom, but none more constant. Some were more popular in their methods, but none weightier. Some were inspired by a livelier faith, but none surpassed him in breadth and depth of conviction. His devotion to the cause was not so much from sympathy with the oppressed individual, as from a profound humanitarian spirit which embraced his kind, and "hated only wrong to man."

"If to the master's plea he gave
   The vast contempt his manhood felt,
He saw a brother in the slave,
   With man as equal man he dwelt."

The fame he acquired among appreciative friends as a scholar, orator and statesman, was greatly augmented by the tribute his enemies paid to his powers by their maledictions. They made that tribute complete, when all their other arguments lying broken about them like pygmies' straws, they brutally struck him down in the Senate chamber.

"Lifted like Saul's above the crowd,
   Upon his kingly forehead fell
The first sharp bolt of slavery's cloud,
   Launched at the truth he urged so well."

Letter from Hon. Charles Sumner:

Senate Chamber
3ᵈ March '72

My dear Sir,

The Underground Rail
road has performed its
part but it must al-
ways be remembered
gratefully as one of the
peculiar institutions
of our country. I can-
not think of it without
a throbbing heart

You do well to com-
memorate those associated
with it by service or
by benefit, the' save
or other saved. The
story of the Late War has
had its "Role of Honor".
You will give us two
other rolls, worthy of
equal honor; — the
roll of fugitives from
Slavery helped on the

way to freedom. & also the
roll of their self-sacrificing bene-
factors. I always hesitated which
to honor most, the fugitive slave
or the citizen who helped him
in defiance of unjust laws. Your
book will teach us to honor both.
Accept my best wishes, &
believe me, My dear Sir
very faithfully Yours
Charles Sumner

Letter from Hon. Henry Wilson:

> Senate Chamber
> March, 2nd 1872.
>
> My Dear Mr Still,
>
> I have glanced over a few pages of your History of the Underground Rail Road, and I must earnestly commend it. You have done a good work. This story of the heroic conduct of Fugitives & oppression, and of the devotion of their friends

will be read with deep
interest, especially by the
old friends of the
slave in the stern
struggle through which
we have passed. I hope
your labors will be
rewarded by a grateful
public.

Yours Truly

Henry Wilson

This letter, easily and gracefully written, and manifest-
ing the kindest disposition, is the reflex of the man. Its
author was the warmest-hearted friend the colored race ever
had. His advocacy of all anti-slavery measures was earnest
and able. Not so learned as his illustrious colleague in the
Senate, he was never embarrassed by theories, but dealt
homely, trenchant blows for the cause in such a way as to
secure him the respect of friends and enemies alike. He was

preeminently wise in his selection of time and methods. The good he was capable of doing was never impaired by hasty action or indiscreet speech. Grave and politic, he got down close to vital principles, and left impressions which a loftier oratory or more florid rhetoric might have failed to make. Great in deliberative influence, high in position, he was not separated from the masses, but was perhaps the most popular, really sympathetic, and truly representative great man the country has ever produced.

The book received the favorable endorsement of the press and met the approval of the friends of the colored race everywhere. On receipt of the first complete copy sent out, that grand anti-slavery pioneer and veteran, William Lloyd Garrison, wrote him as follows:

Roxbury, April 7, 1872

Dear Mr. Still:—I have already delayed too long in thanking you for your presentation to me of your voluminous and well-executed work, *The Underground Railroad*. I have examined it with a deep and thrilling interest. It is a most important portion of antislavery history, which but for your industry, research, and personal experience and knowledge, might nearly all have been lost to posterity. Its reliableness, moreover, cannot be called in question. It is, therefore, not "fiction founded upon fact," and embellished by a lively imagination, but fact without a particle of fiction, narrated in a simple, ingenuous straightforward manner, and needing no coloring whatever. What a revelation it makes of the barbarities of the slave system, of the formidable obstacles which interposed to prevent a successful exodus from the house of bondage, of the terrible exposures and sufferings to which the fugitive slaves were subjected in their attempts to be free, of the daring and heroism required to run the risk of betrayal, recapture, starvation in the swamp, and drowning in the river, suffocation in the box, seizure by the two-legged and four-legged bloodhounds in hot pursuit, and a thousand other perils. How it illustrates, too, the abject subservience of the nation to the slave power, so that even in Boston the atrocious Fugitive Slave Law was as effectually enforced as it could have been in New Orleans; and in all our broad domains none could give shelter or assistance to the hunted and famishing victim, except at the peril of fine and imprisonment! And yet, numerous as are the instances you have recorded, they are only samples of thousands of others which can never be chronicled, running through six generations. May we trust our senses that there is an end of all this wickedness—that a final and marvelous deliverance has been wrought for all in bondage? Yes, it is true, and there has been the same divine interposition as of old. "And the Lord said, I have surely seen the affliction of my people which are in Egypt, and have heard their cry by reason of their taskmasters; for I know their sorrows, and I am come down to deliver them out of the hand of the Egyptians. . . . Thy right hand, O Lord, is become glorious in power; thy right hand, O Lord, hath dashed in pieces the enemy."

I hope that the sale of your work will be largely extended, not only that the large expense incurred by its preparation and printing may be liberally covered, but for the enlightenment of the rising generations as to the inherent cruelty of the defunct slave system, and to perpetuate such an abhorrence of it as to prevent any further injustice toward the colored population of our land. It is a book for every household.

> Yours with best wishes,

WILLIAM STILL   WILLIAM LLOYD GARRISON

In the same spirit wrote J. Miller McKim, another of the staunchest and most active friends the anti-slavery cause ever had:

Lewellyn Park, March 15, 1872

Dear William:—I received your book last evening and have since been reading it with feelings of mingled pleasure and pride; pleasure at the valuable contribution which it furnishes to anti-slavery history and anti-slavery literature, and pride that you are the author of it.

The sketches—one of which does me too much honor—are as a whole in good taste and, with hardly an exception, sufficiently brief, and, except in my own case, not too strongly drawn.

But the chief value of the book will be found in its main narratives, which illustrate to the life the character of slavery, the spirit and temper of the men engaged for its overthrow, and the difficulties which had to be overcome by these men in the accomplishment of their purpose.

A book so unique in kind, so startling in interest, and so trustworthy in its statements, cannot fail to command a large reading now and in the generations yet to come. That you, my long-time friend and associate, are the author of this book is to me a matter of great pride and delight. I thank you very much for the copy you have sent me and for the added honor you have done me in serving me next after the "old pioneer." When you forward the next copy have the goodness to put your autograph on the fly leaf.

Yours ever faithfully,
J. M. McKim

No tribute to the work was more welcome than that of the Rev. Dr. Furness, who had given so much of his valuable time to the reading of the proof sheets:

PHILADELPHIA, February 23, 1872

Having read this record of *The Underground Railroad*, I can only say that it is a work of extraordinary interest and of great value as an illustration of the terrible despotism, which a little while ago reigned over us all, and which is now (thank heaven!) no more.

WILLIAM H. FURNESS, D. D.

To WILLIAM STILL

Mr. Greeley expressed his appreciation of the book in the following characteristic letter, a lithographic *fac simile* of which is presented to show his peculiar handwriting. Nor must the reader, especially if he or she be one from whose neck the heavy yoke of slavery was lifted, look upon it for the purpose of gratifying curiosity alone. It must be remembered that in that quaint, almost illegible handwriting first appeared those scathing arraignments of the slave system, and those masterly arguments in behalf of universal freedom which caused the *Tribune* to rank as first among anti-slavery papers and made its editor's name beloved among the oppressed and lowly everywhere. Cramped and miserable handwriting you may say; yet what great, ponderous thoughts it was made to convey! The scrawling lines which terrorized the typographist were laden with immortal truth. The ragged, puzzling paragraphs which none but an expert could decipher were, when transferred to the printed page; heated shot fired from liberty's columbiad against the bulwarks of slavery, carrying consternation wherever they struck.

Many profess to find in a man's handwriting an index to his character. They will be disappointed if they search for Mr. Greeley's character in his handwriting. His was an open, frank, unsuspicious nature. His chirography is pinched, hard and difficult. His thoughts flowed freely, his words were apt, his sentences, when not tinged with too much brusqueness, were models of pointed strength and rhetorical neatness. His handwriting is painful in its rough, craggy, bewildering irregularities. No man could mistake Mr. Greeley's sentiments when he spoke or wrote, nor help feeling that they were, in their plainness and force, a part of the earnest man's soul.

(*Translation of above letter.*)

Dear Sir:—For most of the years I have lived, the escape of fugitives from slavery, and their efforts to baffle the human and other bloodhounds who tracked them, formed the romance of American History. That romance is ended, and our grandchildren will hardly believe its leading incidents except on irresistible testimony. I rejoice that you are collecting and presenting that testimony, and heartily wish you a great success.

Never since its publication has it been out of demand. Already it has had a large sale. The author is proud to say in connection with it, that its value to his colored brethren, especially in the South, as a history of what their fathers and mothers were willing to endure for liberty's sake, and as an incentive to further heroic struggle for the emancipation of mind and soul, has been constantly growing, and, without vanity or enthusiasm, it is safe to predict that it will grow, as time multiplies readers and begets appreciation.

HIS BUSINESS LIFE

William Still's business life is touched upon last because it is not yet finished; and again because, in so far as his history furnishes a worthy example to his brethren, it is the most important. It is in this life that, as a man of color, he has struck most directly the prejudices which operated to sustain slavery, and which still operate, though with diminishing force, to retard the progress of his race. It is here, too, that he has had to stem the varying and strong tides of competition with which the arenas of business are filled. Clash with the business world is necessarily trying and severe.

There is no combat which so thoroughly tests the stamina of a man as that waged on the street, in the marts, and wherever trade invites energy, sharpens wit, applauds success, or mercilessly mocks failure. Whoever has gone through the ordeal and come out with laurels is one who has shown qualities which the bulk of mankind respect and approve. And it is safe to say that this respect and approval is in direct ratio to the difficulties which those qualities are called upon to surmount.

Mr. Still's earliest investment in real estate was made soon after he entered the anti-slavery office. He was advised by his friend, Mr. McKim, to buy a lot in West Philadelphia, one of a great number then being introduced to the market, near where the Hon. William D. Kelley now lives. The price was $33. Small as it was, he had to purchase on the installment plan, for funds were then very scarce. By and by the lot was paid for. Year by year it grew in worth, and when, long afterwards, he sold it for $950, he felt some of the pride which springs from a successful business venture. Encouraged by the advance on this lot, he bought others on the same plan, and held them for an increased price.

An episode of his business life which had its sad side sentimentally, yet in a cold, commercial sense its justly retributive side, is not out of place here. Just after his marriage he went to Mr. Cassey, reputed to be the next wealthiest colored man in Philadelphia after Stephen Smith, to rent a little house he had set his heart upon, and which was then vacant. There was no dispute about the price, but the owner's terms were "rent in advance," a rule he never departed from. Not even the argument that he (William) did not get his money in advance availed, so he was forced to go away disappointed. Eighteen years afterwards he bought the residence of Mr. Cassey in which this parley took place, and the little house besides, at sheriff's sale, the splendid estate of the owner having fallen under the hammer.

After leaving the anti-slavery office in 1860, he turned directly toward business affairs, with a larger acquaintance with men, more experience in affairs, and greater confidence in his ability than ever before. What he lacked in special knowledge of branches and substantial capital, he hoped to make up by energy and tact.

The very office he had so long served in, and which had been occupied by the Anti-Slavery Society for nearly a score of years, was about to become vacant. Here was a good point to start from. The dwelling could be used by his family; the room below, which was quite large, could be turned to business account. The building was secured as an initial step. What next? He had worked in a stove store long enough to know how to take stoves apart and put them together; how to repair and burnish; how to buy castings at the foundry and fit them; how to adjust pipe and set stoves in place, and, last but not least, he learned how cheaply stoves sold in the spring and summer, and how high they sold in autumn and winter. Here then was an experience which might be turned to practical account. The business should therefore be that of dealing in second-hand and new stoves. A summer supply, bought cheaply, repaired nicely with his own hands, and supplemented by patterns of new styles from the various foundries with which to take orders, these, with diligence and care to please on his part, made an assuring outlook.

Now as to the capital. He had less than $300 at his command. He had made a few purchases of lots at times, and these had advanced so as to be worth perhaps $2,000, but he did not wish to mortgage them or turn them into cash if he could avoid it. A partner with money, and with other available qualities, was the plan. He tried in vain to find a man willing to share his hopes of success and his risks of failure. Then he added the thought that if he could, by exposing samples, sell enough coal on commission to pay his rent, he might work cautiously into his prospective stove business on his own account. Thus the matter shaped itself, and he was afloat in his little business boat on his little but precarious business sea.

Various were the speculations indulged by older business heads concerning his enterprise. Some predicted failure because he was not sufficiently acquainted with the business to turn all its points to account. Some thought he could never succeed without more capital than he seemed to have at his command. By far the larger number looked upon his venture as hazardous because it was undertaken by a colored man, who would not only have to contend with legitimate competition but also the prejudices against his race.

He had, however, discounted all these sentiments in his own mind. Urbanity, honesty, and aptitude would neutralize his color. Industry, good work, and fair pay would supply him capital. Strict attention to details would speedily supply all he lacked in knowledge of his business.

He could not hire help, but he went into his shop by four in the morning, and burnished, repaired, adjusted and wrought, completing almost half a day's work before the hour of opening for customers. Then, in changed attire, he was ready to attend to the regular trade of the day. Very soon the laws which controlled other men in the same business began to operate in his case. He felt a responsiveness all along the lines of traffic. People did not see or feel his color. The character of his work, promptitude in contract, jealous care of the interests of patrons—these were great arguments, before which prejudices flew as a thief before his pursuers.

In a single month his sales of coal more than paid his rent for three months. Before the end of the year he was not only assured of his own success, but those with whom he had business relations, such as foundrymen and iron-workers and dealers, were entirely willing to extend to him the courtesy of business credit. As he had never asked this, nor even so much as a loan from his old and intimate friends, he did not avail himself of what he no longer needed.

The second year opened auspiciously. Sales of coal largely increased. He felt that he could safely branch out by adding the business of manufacturing. Competent sheet-iron workers were employed to make gas stoves, boilers, range appliances, and to build heaters. At the same time he enlarged his stock of sample castings of new patterns of stoves from the leading foundries. Thus, within, there were the rattle and bustle of prosperous business, and, without, such display of new and tasteful wares as attracted attention. But perhaps the greatest novelty about the store, and the best card, too, was the fact that it was a colored man's enterprise. Appreciation of the fact that here was one of a race whose mission seldom seemed to soar above menial work, or subordinate service, who was succeeding in the avenues of active trade, drew patronage from rich and poor, without respect to nationality.

And yet—such is the peculiarity of prejudice—at the very moment he felt himself free from discrimination as to color, he was compelled to witness, in his own store, a barbaric exhibition of race malignity in an attack upon Prince Rivers, a colored sergeant, who had come on from Charleston on Government business. A colored soldier was, at that time, a novelty in the North, and the sergeant's uniform proved an offence to even the wearers of the same dress in the streets of Philadelphia. The blue was supposed to be dishonored if upon any but white soldiers. The sergeant was pounced upon by a squad of soldiery as an offender against all propriety as to dress and uniform and, in beating a forced retreat, he ran into and through Mr. Still's store in search of a place of safety from his howling and infuriated pursuers. The consequence might have been bloodshed, and even the death of the innocent sergeant, but for the timely and brave intervention of Rev. Mr. Gibbs and others present, who checked the maddened mob and diverted their unmanly and savage aim. In less than a year afterwards the white soldier classed the colored soldier as comrade, the blue befitted both as well, and, actuated by the same patriotic spirit, they marched shoulder to shoulder to a common death or victory. Apropos to this thought, almost at this juncture Mr. Still was visited by Robert Smalls, the colored slave and pilot of the PLANTER (afterwards an M.C. and general of South Carolina State Militia), who ran his ship not, as was intended, against the Union fleet, but directly into it, where its capture, with all on board, became an easy and sure thing. For this heroic act he was highly honored by the government, and his name received favorable mention in every loyal circle.

The third year of business was even more prosperous. He had friends everywhere, and could expand his trade so as to cover all the points of profit. Many of the largest foundrymen, among them Mr. Charles Noble, of the Noble Foundries, felt free to compliment him by saying, that at first they doubted his success, not from lack of energy or integrity, but of knowledge of the business. Now, however, they admitted that their doubts were ill-founded. They informed him of a prospective rise in all the wares he dealt in, on account of the war, and kindly proffered credit to any amount to enable him to stock up in advance. The information he took advantage of, but not the credit, and he realized handsomely on his investment.

In the fourth year of his business career, he was visited by Edward M. Davis, son-in-law of Lucretia Mott, who informed him that he had come to tender him the position of Post Sutler at Camp William Penn, near Jenkintown, some eight miles from Philadelphia. This was an honor so little anticipated, that the announcement quite stunned him. Loss, or at least disorder, of his business would be the penalty of acceptance. His reply was prompt: "I do not want the place. I have worked hard to build up a business, and now that I have succeeded, I do not desire to leave it." "You must take it," was the reply. "The Supervisory Committee has confidence in your ability and integrity, you have worked hard in the cause of freedom, and you are entitled to it. While some of the members are in favor of a white man, we feel sure we can elect you."

Left to think over the proposition, he found reasons for reconsidering his refusal. The stove business was then about over for the season, and perhaps he might get away from camp before the autumn trade began. He was in the draft, and this service would be accepted as equivalent to that of regular enlistment. So he consented to let his name go before the committee, which consisted of some seventy of the staunchest Union citizens. He got all the votes present at the meeting except one, which was thrown, from purely patriotic motives let it be understood, in favor of an applicant who offered $4,000 for the place.

In looking over the situation, he found that the object of the committee and of the commanding officer, Colonel Wagner, in selecting him, was to break up several abuses which had been winked at, if not encouraged by his predecessor, and which tended to demoralize the soldiers. Among these was the smuggling and sale of liquors and of deteriorated goods, jewelry, trinkets and gewgaws. His commission was obtained through Hon. W. D. Kelley, from Hon. Edwin M. Stanton, then Secretary of War, and he entered upon the active duties of the post determined not to disappoint those who had so highly and unexpectedly honored him. He had a hard struggle to break up the demoralizing practices which prevailed, but by persistent efforts he at last succeeded. The soldiers themselves objected to any interference with, what they were pleased to call their freedom, and he was much annoyed by invidious reports and highly spiced slanders circulated by some of the jealous aspirants for the place. One trick of the soldiers would have proved quite costly in the end if it had not been promptly checkmated. They were made the victims of sharpers on their expeditions around town, and often came back to camp with counterfeit money. This they would bring to Mr. Still, and if they failed to pass it on him for regular purchases, they would insist that, as it was what he paid them with, he was bound to redeem it. To avoid all trouble from this source, he ceased to give out any money at all except new and approved notes from the bank. Then he could always answer, "That they could not have obtained worthless paper from him, for he paid out only that which was new and of undoubted quality."

He held this position till the end of the war. His methods met the approval of the Supervisory Committee, and he never failed to secure their hearty cooperation and that of Colonel Wagner in his work of administration. His prices for goods were made the subject of a comparison with similar goods sold in the city stores, and according to the testimony of Colonel R. R. Corson, secretary of the Supervisory Committee, were found to be about as reasonable. The welfare of the colored soldiers, in camp and in the field, was always a matter of great moment to him. His benefactions were frequent and liberal. On one occasion when Mr. Thomas Webster, chairman of the

Supervisory Committee, was making pressing appeals in their behalf for aid, Mr. Still cheerfully tendered his check for $500.

His camp duties were all the while arduous and provocative of much anxiety of mind. Supplemented by those of his stove business, it is evident that he was a very busy man. Regarding these responsibilities which were being successfully met, as a test of practical capacity, it will be seen he had developed business powers of a very high order, and had landed on a plane where they met with full recognition. But business did not cramp and dwarf his other and better life. Engrossed as much as he was, he never forgot his church, his Sunday-school, his charities, nor the cause to which his life had been dedicated, namely, the rights of his race and their progress and elevation. In other words, amid the severe demands of a widely extended and rapidly extending business career, he found time to lead the life of a public-spirited citizen.

As to his race, the war was a shifting of lines of action. Emancipation had brought into view new objects to be attained. The changed situation required that new methods should be pursued. The colored man was a citizen, in a national sense; but as yet, even the most advanced states had not responded to the sentiment of universal citizenship and equal rights for all. Society, even in Quaker Philadelphia, was singularly stubborn in its adherence to the old race distinctions and discriminations. Mr. Still's business, urgent as the business of any man, called him in every direction. He naturally felt aggrieved at the fact that he was denied the privilege of riding in the street cars.

The personal hardship he experienced on account of this privation, as well as what he saw inflicted on others, together with his sentiments respecting it, are so well expressed by an article which he contributed to *The Philadelphia Press*, and which was reproduced in the *National Anti-Slavery Standard*, of the issue of January 2nd, 1864, that we here present it.

THE PASSENGER-CARS
AND COLORED CITIZENS

To the Editor of "The Press:"

Sir:—Please permit me to state through the columns of your liberal journal a matter of very serious public grievance which colored people generally are daily subjected to, and which, as an individual, I experienced to-day to a degree that I shall not attempt to fully describe, although I feel I shall never forget it.

Briefly, the circumstances were these: Being under the necessity of going out to Camp William Penn to-day on business, I took the North Pennsylvania Railroad, and reached the ground about eleven o'clock. Remembering that pressing duties required my presence at my store by a certain hour in the early part of the afternoon, I promptly attended to my business at the camp, but as I could not return by the way I came without waiting two and a half hours for the down train, I concluded that I would walk over to Germantown, and come to the city by the one o'clock steam-cars. Accordingly, I reached Germantown, but too late for the train by about five minutes, as the cars had just gone. To wait another hour I felt was out of the question, hence I decided to take the city passenger-cars. Soon one came along with but few passengers in it, and into it I walked with a man who had been to the camp with me (but fortunately he happened to be of the approved complexion), and took a seat. Quickly the conductor approached me, and I tendered him the fare for us both, the man alluded to being in my employment. The conductor very cordially received the money, but before he took time to hand me the change that was due to me, invited me to "step out on the platform."

"Why is this?" I remarked.

"It is against the rules," he added.

"Who objects?" I inquired.

"It is the aristocracy," he again added.

"Well, it is a *cruel rule!* And I believe this is the only city of note in the civilized world where a decent colored man cannot be allowed to ride in a city passenger-car. Even the cars which were formerly built in Philadelphia for New Orleans were not devoid of accommodations for colored people inside," I continued. "And now, with regard to the aristocracy, I do not believe that the blame rests with them; for I happen to be one of a committee who some time back brought this question before the public in the shape of a petition, and it was very freely signed by hundreds of the most respectable citizens—by leading clergymen, lawyers, doctors, editors, merchants, etc., amongst whom were Bishop Potter, Hon. Horace Binney, etc., and some of the railway presidents besides."

Of course, the conductor declared that he had no objections himself, but continued to insist that it was "the rules."

"Who is the president of this road?" I inquired.

After pausing for a moment (what he meant I know not), he answered by saying he believed his name was "Mr. Whartman."

"A former president," I remarked, "declared to a committee that 'no such rules had ever been made on this road.'"

I told him that I paid taxes, etc., but of course it was all of no avail.

Biding on the platform of a bitter cold day like this I need not say is almost intolerable; but to compel persons to pay the same as those who enjoy comfortable seats inside by a good fire seems quite atrocious.

Yet I felt under the circumstances compelled to submit to the wrong for the sake of arriving at my place of business in due time. But before I arrived at my destination it began to snow, which, as I was already thoroughly chilled with the cold, made the platform utterly intolerable; hence I concluded to walk the rest of the distance, and accordingly got off, feeling satisfied that nowhere in Christendom could be found a better illustration of Judge Taney's decision in the Dred Scott case, in which he declared that "black men have no rights which white men are bound to respect," than are demonstrated by the "rules" of the passenger-cars of the City of Brotherly Love.

The judge's decision and the "rules" have harassed me every moment since. I try to think of cannibals in heathen lands and traitors in the South, and wrongs generally, but it is all to no purpose; this car inhumanity sticks to me.

"But this is only an individual case, hence but a trifling matter," you may think, Mr. Editor. Far from it, sir. Every colored man, woman, and child of the entire 25,000 inhabitants of this city, many of whom are tax-payers and as upright as any other class of citizens, are daily liable to this treatment. The truth is, so far as my case is concerned, I fared well compared with the treatment some have received. A long catalogue of injuries and outrages could be recounted, but suffice it to remind your readers of only one or two instances:

A venerable old minister of the Gospel, in going from here to his home at Frankford, one dark, cold, and rainy night last winter, while occupying the only place on the platform assigned for colored people, was killed. Who has forgotten this fact?

One more instance, and I will relieve you. One evening, in going home from a lecture, two elegantly dressed young women stepped into a car and took seats. The conductor courageously brought the rules forward, and one of them instantly stepped out, while the other remained. The car was stopped, and the conductor seized her, and actually, by physical force, thrust her out of the car. The father of this young woman pays several hundred dollars in taxes annually, keeps his horse and carriage, and lives as nicely as most respectable citizens. But the God-given hue of the skin of his daughter rendered her obnoxious to the rules of the railway company, and she had to meekly submit to the outrage.

Respectfully, WILLIAM STILL

Philadelphia, December 11, 1863

Shortly after its publication he was met one morning by Mr. E. M. Davis, who asked him if he had seen his article on the car question as reproduced in the London *Times*. "No," was the answer. The reply was, "Then go to the Merchants' Exchange, and you will find it on file." He found it there, together with a correspondence from Rev. Moncure D. Conway, in which the reverend gentleman took occasion to note that it was one of only two American articles deemed worthy of publication in "The Thunderer" of that issue, and that "it had done the Union cause more harm than a defeat in Virginia."

Notwithstanding such a sentiment from a source so eminent, he did not regret the publication, but deemed the time most opportune to force the battle for his own and the rights of others. Only a few nights afterwards, his convictions were strengthened by an appeal from William H. Scott, R. M. Robinson, and J. F. Wallace to go their bail, they having been arrested and thrust into the lock-up for attempting to ride on the cars contrary to rule. After a long search for the alderman who had committed them, he found him about midnight in bed, and, entering bond for their appearance at court, had them released.

Hard as the discrimination appeared in his own case, its injustice and inhumanity were magnified a thousand-fold by the consideration that it was a visitation, daily and nightly, on all of his color, without regard to weather, distance, time, sex, or age. But personal, or, if you please, race convenience was the least part of the matter. There was a great principle involved, and, consequently, a battle to be fought. He felt sure of a sentiment in the city and everywhere sufficiently strong to operate as a corrective if it could be gotten together and made to pronounce itself. He determined to gather it together, and try the effect of its aggregation.

As a member of the Social and Statistical Society, whose organization and object are hereafter alluded to, he proposed to get up a petition setting forth the wrongs complained of, to be signed by leading representative men in all the various callings. The society adopted this plan, and appointed him, in connection with J. C. White,

J. C. Wears, Rev. J. C. Gibbs, and S. Morgan Smith, to attend to the important work. During his leisure time, for three or four months, he circulated his petition among merchants, manufacturers, lawyers, doctors, ministers, and prominent men of every calling. The response was even heartier than he had anticipated. Such an array of truly representative names had, in all probability, never been gathered together in any cause in a single city. Such was the number and such their weight, that it was often called into requisition on other important occasions, as, for instance, when a great meeting of leading citizens was held to denounce the proscription, when the Union League was about to be organized, and when afterwards members of the League sought to influence the minds of legislators against race discriminations.

One of the many incidents connected with the labor of obtaining signers is worthy of record. He was invited by a reverend gentleman belonging to the Methodist Preachers' Association to visit that body in its organized capacity. The invitation was accepted, and on the next Monday morning he was promptly on hand at the Union church, Fourth Street between Market and Arch, with his great petition. The gentleman who had invited him made known his errand. He had hardly finished his remarks before a small-sized, bushy-haired preacher was on his feet, looking all primed for a hot contest, who very significantly said, "I should like to know if this petition has been brought before any similar body?" A gentleman, who evidently understood the motive of the interrogator, and who feared that a negative answer would encourage him to open his batteries, endeavored to throw him off the track by a short speech. Catching the drift of things, Mr. Still followed him with a request that leave be granted him to answer the question. This being readily accorded, he made the announcement that he had not come for the purpose of creating confusion or provoking argument, and proceeded to say, "I have visited the Episcopal rooms, and there met Bishop Potter and a number of Episcopal clergymen. They all unhesitatingly signed my petition. I have visited the Baptist Association, and they all unhesitatingly affixed their signatures." This was enough.

Just then one of the ministers present shouted, "And I will sign it with a John Randolph signature!"

The moderator said: "If you will wait till the meeting dispatches its routine business, I have no doubt many will sign it; as for myself, I will be glad to do it."

At the close of the meeting nearly all that large body of ministers came forward and signed, and, at Mr. Still's request, affixed to their names that of the church over which they presided. While this spontaneous movement was going on, the little, bushy-headed preacher, who had attempted to baffle the work, was beating an inglorious retreat by way of the back door.

The work involved in getting up this monster petition was so great, and the results to his race which hung upon it so momentous, as to warrant its appearance in the history of a life of which it of itself forms a conspicuous chapter. Before presenting it, however, it needs to be said that, after the odious distinction it sought to remove was abolished, the secretary of the Pennsylvania Historical Society solicited it, in order to give it a place among the archives of that venerable institution. And there it remains to this day, a curious relic of the times when slavery, though dead in fact, still lived a life of detestable legacies.

PETITION FOR THE COLORED PEOPLE OF PHILADELPHIA TO RIDE IN THE CARS

To the Board of Managers of the various City Passenger Cars:
The colored citizens of Philadelphia suffer very serious inconvenience and hardship daily by being excluded from riding in the city passenger cars. In New York City, and in all the principal Northern cities, except Philadelphia, they ride. Even in New Orleans (although subject to some proscription) they ride in the cars. Why then should they be excluded in Philadelphia—in a city standing so pre-eminently high for its benevolence, liberality, love of freedom and Christianity as the city of Brotherly Love?

Colored people pay more taxes here than is paid by the same class in any other Northern city. The members of the *Social and Statistical Association*, although numbering less than fifty members, pay annually about five thousand dollars into the tax-collector's office.

Therefore, the undersigned respectfully petition that the various Boards of the city passenger cars rescind the rules indiscriminately excluding colored persons from the inside of the cars.

Among the hundreds of distinguished and representative signers were:

HORACE BINNEY,	ELI K. PRICE,
BISHOP POTTER,	REV. J. MORTON, D.D.,
JUDGE GEORGE M. STROUD,	DR. S. S. WHITE,
BENJAMIN COATES,	CHARLES GIBBONS,
M. W. BALDWIN,	REV. PHILLIPS BROOKS,
REV. JAMES S. DICKINSON,	JAMES A. WRIGHT,
REV. J. NEWTON BROWN,	M. B. GRIER,
FRANCIS R. COPE,	JOSEPH S. LOVERING,
JOHN P. CROZER,	JOHN SARTAIN,
HENRY C. CAREY,	MORTON MCMICHAEL,
CHARLES GILPIN,	B. P. HUNT,
EDWARD OLMSTED,	REV. J. WHEATON SMITH,
CONSTANTINE HERING, M.D.,	JOHN WEIGAND,
REV. WILLIAM H. FURNESS,	TOWNSEND SHARPLESS, etc.

When it was completed, and the time became ripe, Mr. Still was granted the privilege of presenting it in person, in connection with the Committee, to the Board of Railway Presidents, at the Merchants' Exchange. He did so in a speech appropriate to the occasion, whose effect was entirely favorable. Every moral, legal and political point had been carried. There was nothing left to contend with but a weak line of what was pleasingly called policy, but which was in reality a relic of prejudice, which, once in the heart of a custom-bound corporation, is not readily eradicated.

The petition was soon afterwards followed by a strong address, written by Mr. Still and presented in the name of his Committee. In a condensed form it read as follows:

To the Board of Presidents of the City Passenger Railroads:

GENTLEMEN: Since our petition was first presented, New York has removed every vestige of proscription from all the city passenger cars—although the rules of her roads, long before this final change, carried colored people generally, without proscription, except two roads. In these exceptional cases they could ride in cars especially designated by the words "colored people are allowed," etc.

Can it be possible that there is more prejudice and less humanity in Philadelphia than in New York? We cannot think so; and our experience in this very matter of procuring signatures to the petition now under consideration fully justifies us in assuming this ground. We applied to the men who had never rendered themselves publicly obnoxious by advocating anti-slavery or abolition views; men filling the highest positions in the churches, in the legal profession, in the mercantile calling, and in the editorial vocation, and to our great gratification we rarely applied in vain. Amongst the signatures may be found a number of Episcopal clergymen. Not a man of that order to whom we applied hesitated a moment about signing it, but all freely gave their names. Also among the names may be found the pastors of nearly all the leading Methodist churches in this city, who, with one accord, cheerfully furnished their names, and the names of the churches over which they presided, to give additional weight thereto. Every Baptist clergyman also to whom it was presented gave his name and unqualified approval of the measure. Other denominations to whom it was presented signed with equal freedom, so far as they were called upon. Hence we take it for granted that, so far as the public are concerned, should the oppressive and prescriptive rules be changed today, the great majority of the citizens of Philadelphia would acquiesce in the change. And we would further add, in this connection, we are fully persuaded that, if the Board should feel inclined to test this question by allowing any ordinarily decent colored woman to ride on any one of the roads, by an impromptu vote of the passengers, two-thirds would side with the woman as often as the trial may be made. But you may ask, "Will not the vulgar and the lower order of society rebel against colored people riding?" We reply, "No; no sooner here than in New York, Washington or New Orleans."

The truth is, the colored people, in meeting with insults and vulgar epithets from the vulgar, cannot fail to observe that these abuses are, in a great degree, traceable to severe and inhuman rules of this kind.

Nobody insults a colored man or woman in the tax-receiver's office, however full it may be. Nobody insults a colored man or woman in entering a store, even though it may be the most fashionable in the city. Why, then, should the fear exist that the very people who are meeting with colored people in various other directions without insulting them should instantly become so intolerably incensed as to indicate a terrible aspect in this particular?

We say, fearless of successful gainsaying, that the rules of which the colored people of Philadelphia complain in point of severity stand unparalleled, compared with the legislation of any other large city. The fifteen hundred wounded soldiers who lay in pain at the Summit and Satterlee Hospitals a few weeks since received but few visits from their colored brethren, simply because the rules enforced on these cars would not allow decent colored people to ride, and eight or nine dollars per day (the usual charge for carriage hire) was beyond the means of the masses to pay. Yet, we repeat, by the regulations of the city passenger railways, not one mother, wife or sister could be admitted, even to see a United States soldier, a relative, although the presence and succor of such mother, wife or sister might save a life.

It is well known that, through the efforts of the Supervisory Committee of this city, ten or eleven regiments of colored men have been raised for the United States service, and not a few of these brave men have already won imperishable honor on the battlefield. Nevertheless, thrice the number that have been thus raised for the defense of the country are daily and hourly compelled to endure all the outrages and inconveniences consequent upon rules so severe and inexorable as those which have hitherto governed the roads of Philadelphia.

In conclusion, permit us to express the earnest hope that our efforts will this time meet with a more favorable result than before, and that not many weeks or months shall have passed ere such changes will be made as shall remove the cause of complaint for the future.

Respectfully yours,
William Still
Isaiah C. Wears } Committee
S.M. Smith
J.C. Gibbs

The result of these appeals and this great warfare was the removal of the offensive discriminations practiced by managers of public conveyances. It was a victory of which Mr. Still was justly proud, for it not only secured the rights his people were entitled to under the laws, but every step toward it vindicated his judgment, that the prejudicial sentiment to be combated was not a sentiment at all, except among the ignorant, but rather a spirit of carelessness or indifference on the part of those who felt, as soon as their attention was called to the existing evil, that they had been neglecting an important public duty. They were simply a non-assertive civic or political force, which only needed coherence and motion to be irresistible.

As striking deeper into the roots of prejudice, and by way of making example a teacher in behalf of his race, he helped to organize and became corresponding secretary and chairman of the committee of arrangements of a society whose name could be used to secure famous lecturers on topics of citizenship, race relations, human rights, etc. Concert Hall was secured, and a series of lectures provided for during the winter of 1864 to 1865. Many notables responded, among whom were William Lloyd Garrison, General Howard, Frederick Douglass, Hon. Hugh L. Bond, Theodore Tilton, Rev. Sella Martin, Carl Schurz, Jno. M. Langston, Mrs. F. E. W. Harper, and Hon. W. D. Kelley. But the object embraced more than brilliant talks on momentous and living subjects. Sale and gift of tickets were pushed into every society so as to secure as full a representation as possible of the city officials, bar and pulpit representatives, and prominent civilians on the platform, and at the same time present an audience as thoroughly mixed as if race, color, or previous condition had never served as a line of distinction or as groundwork for a prejudice. There was to be no begging for talent, but full pay for every lecturer. The plan was heartily applauded and the project was a success in every particular. The nightly representation on the platform was surprisingly large, and the audiences were always full, promiscuous, and appreciative. The course closed with the society's exchequer overflowing. It was a great winter's work. The races could commingle as equals in search of "the true, the beautiful and the good," without too violent a jar to ancient customs and inherited sentiments. In obedience to new and broader notions of humanity, why could they not do so in the marts, on the thoroughfares, in the shops, in the fields, in deliberative assemblies, and wherever duty called upon manhood to show its strength and meet its solemn responsibilities? The grand result was progress of a most decisive kind. The eight or nine hundred dollars netted by the winter's course were donated to the sick and wounded soldiers in South Carolina, to the aid of destitute freedmen in different parts of the South, and to attorney fees for the prosecution of cases relating to the rights of colored men to ride in the street cars.

The society conducted a second and third course of lectures as successfully as the first. In opening the fourth course it was compelled to move to Market Street Hall, a far less favorable place. Here it had to contend with several non-paying nights on account of the weather, and a failure of one of the speakers—General B. F. Butler—to fulfill his engagement. This course closed, despite energetic effort on the part of the management, with a deficit of some eight or nine hundred dollars, one-half of which Mr. Still offered to pay if the members would raise the balance. About thirty raised as much as $150, and all the rest fell on Mr. Still's shoulders to pay.

Considered as to time, this failure, which was kept a secret, was most inopportune, for what was known as The Social and Statistical Association had been formed, and it had counted on material aid from the lectures. The object of this association, of whose committee of management Mr. Still was chairman, was to gather from every source information respecting the freedmen, and prepare it in succinct form for presentation to senators, representatives and public men everywhere, who might need it or would be likely to use it, in pressing the cause of universal suffrage, the protection of the freedmen, and all such measures as grew out of colored citizenship or tended to establish its rights. Though the work of the association was impaired, it still proved important. It encouraged sentiment, collected much valuable data, and became known as a source whence to draw, when prompt information on the subjects which appertained to it were under discussion. The propriety, if not necessity, for its existence was brought to view by a lament of Hon. Judge Kelley, that there existed an indifference as to the matter of suffrage, and by his suggestion that a meeting should be called in Philadelphia to awaken a keener interest in the momentous subject. Such meeting was called. A committee was appointed to raise money for the distribution of documents and the spread of information. Mr. Still became its chairman. The work was pushed with energy, and soon some $1,260 were raised exclusively from colored people and forwarded to Mr. Kelley. All such work the association, after its organization, assumed.

About the close of the war, when every matter connected with citizenship, suffrage, and the rights and advancement of the colored race formed a conspicuous topic, Mr. Still was visited by Mr. Thomas Webster, who came to inquire as to whether or not colored men were numerous depositors in Savings and other banks, without any identity in the management of the same, and whether it would not prove a source of encouragement to them, and inure greatly to their pecuniary welfare and business importance, if a bank were founded in whose management their capital should find representation. After Mr. Still answered the first part of his question affirmatively, and assented entirely to the theory advanced in the second part, Mr. Webster, in a spirit of enthusiasm, proceeded to propose a bank, one half of whose directors should be white, the other half colored. He had no doubt that prominent men would be glad to take stock in it, and he was sure it would give the colored race a business prestige they could secure in no other way so effectively.

Somewhat captivated with his logic, Mr. Still agreed to move in the matter, at least so far as to provoke inquiry and test sentiment. He invited twenty-five colored men to meet a number of white men and talk over the project. The result of the meeting was a committee, of which Mr. Still was chairman, to further inquire into the subject. He invited Mr. John W. Torrey, the President of the Corn Exchange Bank, who came and spent an evening at the house of Mr. Stephen Smith, where the entire subject of banking, the responsibilities of directorship, the qualities requisite for successful management, the importance of capable and honest clerical aid, were gone over before the committee, very much to their enlightenment and quite to their surprise at the order of talent and intricate machinery necessary to insure profitable investment and handsome dividends. To his great regret, and to that of the rest of the committee, a report had to be framed which was adverse to the project. Granting all the arguments as to benefits likely to accrue to his race, if once the ideal bank were on a sure foundation, he saw in his midst a dearth of colored men who had, up to that time, developed sufficient business capacity to successfully undertake a management of such delicacy and moment. The scheme was in advance of the talent essential to its success. So his report said, in substance, worthy as to conception, plausible as to argument, but inopportune as to time. Thus ended the proposition so far as Philadelphia was concerned. The same matter was simultaneously broached in other parts, and in Washington it took the form of the Freedman's Bank, whose after history and failure confirmed Mr. Still's previous judgment—a judgment he was often rebuked for giving expression to.

Among the other charitable and philanthropic organizations with which Mr. Still was connected, many of them active at this period in his history, and some of them founded to meet the new order of things which concerned, and thought which centered in, his race, was the Freedmen's Aid Union and Commission, with Bishop Simpson as its president, and among its managers such men as William Lloyd Garrison, Chief-Justice Chase, J. Miller McKim, etc. In this mission Mr. Still and Bishop D. A. Payne were chosen as their representatives of the colored race.

Soon after this the Home for Aged and Infirm Colored People had its origin, and here again Mr. Still's services were required as one of its contributors and managers. For a number of years he has been vice president and chairman of the board of managers, and, ever since its foundation, has been a member of the board. For fifteen years scarcely a Sabbath morning passed that did not find him with the old people of the home, reading the Bible to them, and cheering their age in various ways. He was likewise called upon to help organize the Colored Soldiers' and Sailors' Orphans' Home, to which he was a liberal contributor in the purchase of their property, and has ever since been one of its trustees. For years he has been a member of the trustee board of the Home for Destitute Colored Children, and a trustee of Storer College, at Harper's Ferry, instituted in honor of the old hero, John Brown. In all the after work of The Pennsylvania Society for Promoting the Abolition of Slavery, the Relief of Negroes Unlawfully held in Bondage, and for Improving the Condition of the African Race, he has never lost his interest, as this brief history shows, and in 1875, when the society celebrated its centennial, with Vice President Henry Wilson among the distinguished speakers, Mr. Still was chairman of the committee of arrangements.

We ought not to close the instances which serve to illustrate the kind side of his nature without mention of his entertainment to William Lloyd Garrison. This was soon after the close of the war, when the great question of emancipation had been settled, and Mr. Garrison stood laurel-crowned amid the army of worthies who had so nobly defended the castles of freedom, and boldly hurled destructive argument amid assaulting ranks. Of him Mr. Still could safely say with Whittier:

"I love thee with a brother's love,
  I feel my pulses thrill,
To mark thy spirit soar above
  The cloud of human ill.
My heart hath leaped to answer thine,
  And echo back thy words,
As leaps the warrior's at the shine
  And flash of kindred swords."

Out of admiration for the brave man's zeal and power, and with a sense of gratitude for the good he had done to him and his race, Mr. Still tendered him an entertainment at his house, the participants in which were to be Mr. Garrison's friends and admirers, without respect to color. The invitation was accepted in a letter sent through his friend, Mr. McKim, an evening was appointed, and the distinguished guest was promptly on hand. Among the invited friends to greet him were Benjamin Coates, Dillwyn Parish, Joshua L. Hallowell, Henry M. Laing and wife, Passmore Williamson and wife, Miss Sarah Pugh, Alfred H. Love, Miss Mary Grew, Joseph M. Truman, Jr., John D. Stockton, Charles Wise, Mrs. Sarah M. Douglass, Dr. I. Newlin Pierce, Henry Jones and wife, and a host of others. Mr. Garrison was in fine spirits, and the evening was most enjoyably spent. Nor did Mr. Still's gratitude for this beloved man's services end here. When the "Executive Committee of the National Testimonial to William Lloyd Garrison," headed by Governor John A. Andrews, of Massachusetts, was making its effort (unsolicited by Mr. Garrison, if not unknown) to raise a purse of fifty thousand dollars, he found an opportunity to do him further honor by contributing one hundred dollars, which was duly receipted for by Samuel May, Jr., secretary and assistant treasurer of said committee.

In order to take up the thread of his strictly business career, which was dropped, or partially so, in following him through his camp life and in making mention of his philanthropic work, we must go back to the close of the war (1865), where we left him in possession of an attractive store and flourishing trade. Turning again to business, he sought to buy the store property with the view of enlarging his trade. In this he did not succeed, owing to the refusal of the owner to sell. He was not sorry over this, for he felt that there was still a great work for him to do in connection with his race, and that the enlargement of his business responsibilities would curtail his power to do it agreeably or effectively.

That he might have better opportunity to attend to this work of amelioration, he concluded to seek an outlet from some of his cares by addressing himself directly to the business of selling coal, first securing a party in the stove store who might prove capable of its management. He advertised in the anti-slavery papers, corresponded with many friends, and sought in various ways and in all available places for such a man, but, notwithstanding the fact that he offered store and stock on the easiest terms, he could not succeed, to his great surprise, in finding one. In this he was made more than ever to feel the need of colored men turning their attention to trades and business.

Meanwhile, he was looking for a suitable spot on which to build a coal yard. Hearing that some lots were in the market on Washington Avenue between Twelfth and Thirteenth Streets, he went to see them, and found that they would suit his purposes. We must here give in detail the adventure attending his purchase, as, if he interpreted the situation correctly, it was the only time in all his business career he was made to personally feel that his color was a hindrance to his enterprise.

Selecting one of the lots, he went to the real-estate agent, Samuel Kirkpatrick, on Fourth above Walnut, to negotiate for its purchase. Terms were agreed upon, and an advance was tendered to clinch the bargain, which was declined. He was told to come again the next day, to make the payment and get the deed. He was on hand at the hour appointed, but, to his great disappointment, was told that he could not have the lot. On asking for a reason, none was given that appeared at all valid. A flimsy excuse or two was offered for the shabby violation of agreement, such as, "It was feared the neighbors might give trouble," and that was all. Suppressing his chagrin, he did not stop to parley, but went away, determined in his mind to have it. Going directly to Dr. S. S. White, he told him the circumstance, and concluded by saying that he wanted him to go and buy it. The doctor called his brother James, and the three went to a conveyancer, who was instructed to make the purchase in the doctor's name. Although he acted promptly, he was informed that the lot was sold. An adjoining lot, larger than the first, remained. This was purchased by the doctor. The deed was made out to him, and before being placed on record was duly transferred to Mr. Still. Thus possessed of a desirable site, he built capacious sheds, laid the necessary railroad tracks, and altogether erected such improvements as were a credit to his surroundings and the entire street.

Feeling that no exception could be taken to his taste at least, he stocked his yard and embarked almost immediately on an active, paying business. By careful attention to details; by using good teams and judicious help; by dealing honestly and promptly with those who furnished as well as those who bought, he has had the satisfaction of seeing his business grow every year since its foundation, and of numbering among his patrons every class and nationality. As in the stove business, he speedily passed the point where even the lowest prejudice made itself felt, either in dealing with him or refusing to deal with him. Even the real estate broker who had refused to sell him a site for his yard came afterwards upon his premises to congratulate him on his improvements and his prosperity, and to convey to him the best wishes of the former owner of the land, Mrs. Judge Peters, who had not heard that he was the purchaser till six months after the transfer. And, as in his former business, he finds that this one advertises itself. The passerby stops to look at the neat appearance of things, and to make complimentary remark. The newspapers mention his enterprise favorably. For instance, *The Press* thus:

"A GOOD PLACE TO GET COAL.—Mr. William Still has now the finest coal yard on Washington Avenue, fitted up by himself with an office, a stable, a car track, and all the appurtenances and needs of a first-class coal depot. Everything seems to be constructed in the most substantial manner, wearing a neat, attractive appearance. His coal is of good quality, and is furnished to dealers on liberal terms."

His customers, finding themselves dealt with fairly, promptly, and in precisely such a spirit as meets their ideal of business responsibility and enterprise, adhere to him, and kindly exercise an influence in his behalf. His old friends, endeared to him by long association in the cause of his race, rejoice to see him working out his business problem with hands as dexterous as though they were white, and with results as sure as though commercial methods and manners had been within reach of his race for generations.

The entire business plane is open for him to move about upon with the freedom that attaches to integrity, energy, urbanity, and good financial credit, and with only the restraints that are speedily and inexorably imposed upon all men, without respect to rank or condition, who lack those essential qualities or violate those vital principles. Among the men of his calling he has secured an identity as clearly defined and as free from limitation as any. He negotiates as advantageously as his companion capitalists; his credit brings to him the same benefits, his shipments are as promptly attended to, his patronage as warmly solicited. In the casual trips of the coal fraternity to the coal regions for purpose of business and pleasure, he alone is made master of the limit to companionship and social intermingling. And it is so at the banks, in the counting-houses, and wherever men group themselves in business trial, or assemble in competitive quest of fortune. Without knowing how, why, or by whom his name was proposed, he received the usual letter of solicitation to become a member of the Philadelphia Board of Trade from its executive committee, and was afterwards duly notified that he was a unanimously elected member. Thus he has, for years, moved smoothly and creditably over his business career, reaping the rewards of energy and integrity in the shape of a daily enlarging confidence, a firmer and broader status, a growing ability to meet his duties as head of an interesting family, as an active church worker (for many years an elder in the Presbyterian church), as a philanthropic and public-spirited citizen.

At the Centennial Exhibition (1876), he entered a handsome exhibit of his book, bound in various styles of binding. It attracted much attention as an evidence of good taste, and as being one of the few exhibits on hand calculated to show what the colored race were doing in arts and the industries. By this consideration he was entitled to and obtained, of course, all the rights and privileges of all other exhibitors, without regard to his color.

In person, Mr. Still is above the average height, of square, strong build, and, though past sixty years of age, is as vigorous and active as a man of forty-five. His features are regular. His forehead is high and well-shaped. His entire facial expression is pleasant, intellectual, and indicative of strong character. In manner he is easy and gentlemanly, and in speech soft, direct and fluent.

HIS CHILDREN

His children are four in number, two girls and two boys. They were born at a time when prejudice against the colored race was active even in Philadelphia, and when the opportunities for obtaining a good education were comparatively limited. He desired that they should have all the facilities which could be afforded, and, not finding those near or around him, he often thought of removing to Canada till they were grown and their education was completed. Indeed, at this period, owing to the vindictiveness of the pro-slavery element, and his identity with abolition, he did not know at what moment he might be compelled to flee beyond the border in order to save his own life and the lives of his wife and children.

But year after year passed, and he was permitted to remain. The light of liberty grew brighter, and the howls of the "Killers," "Schuylkill Rangers," "Bouncers," "Plug Uglies," "Rioters," "Slave Hunters," and the ungodly, proscriptive element, by whatever name known, grew fainter and fainter in the forests of ignorance. His eldest child, Caroline Virginia, was sent to the Friends' Institute for Colored Youth for several years, and until she was sufficiently advanced to take a higher course. She was then sent to Oberlin College, Ohio, where she spent four years, all the while residing in the family of Professor Peck, a highly esteemed professor in the institution. She graduated in the summer of 1868, with a class of forty-four members, and was the only colored graduate and youngest member. At the anniversary of the Ladies' Literary Society, held during the commencement, she was elected to preside, an honor probably never before conferred upon one of her race under similar circumstances.

After graduating, she returned to Philadelphia and taught for a time in the House of Industry, one of the many noble charities of the city. This occupation did not satisfy her ambitions, and she turned her attention to the study of medicine, with a view to entering in active practice. After years of study in the Medical Department of Howard University and in the Female Medical College of Philadelphia, she again graduated, and this time with a full professional diploma. Going to Boston, she spent one year as hospital physician. Returning to her native city, she began regular practice and is still engaged in it.

The second child, William Wilberforce, was educated at Lincoln University, Pennsylvania, where he ranked among the honor men. On graduating, he delivered the mathematical oration, and three years afterwards the master's oration. Desiring to turn his attention to business, he afterwards completed a course of commercial accounts under the supervision of Samuel W. Crittenden, from whom he received a certificate of proficiency.

The third child, Frances Ellen, received her preliminary education at the Institute for Colored Youth at Philadelphia, and afterwards attended Oberlin College. She then took a normal course in a kindergarten institution, which qualified her to teach. She is now teaching a kindergarten school in Philadelphia.

The fourth child, Robert George, is at present (1883) a member of the senior class in Lincoln University, with a prospect of graduating in June.

Here ends the narrative of a life which, beginning in a lowly way and progressing amid difficulties, grew into good and noble uses. It is a life yet full of possibilities. Let us hope that it will be spared for even better and nobler uses.

Appendices

Pages 37 – 38 from *Underground Rail Road Records*, 1886.

THE SEPARATION

With regard to Peter's separation from his mother, when a little boy, in few words, the facts were these: His parents, Levin and Sidney, were both slaves on the Eastern Shore of Maryland. "I will die before I submit to the yoke," was the declaration of his father to his young master before either was twenty-one years of age. Consequently he was allowed to buy himself at a very low figure, and he paid the required sum and obtained his "free papers" when quite a young man—the young wife and mother remaining in slavery under Saunders Griffin, as also her children, the latter having increased to the number of four, two little boys and two little girls. But to escape from chains, stripes, and bondage, she took her four little children and fled to a place near Greenwich, New Jersey. Not a great while, however, did she remain there in a state of freedom before the slave-hunters pursued her, and one night they pounced upon the whole family, and, without judge or jury, hurried them all back to slavery. Whether this was kidnapping or not is for readers to decide for themselves.

Safe back in the hands of her owner, to prevent her from escaping a second time, every night for about three months she was cautiously "kept locked up in the garret," until, as they supposed, she was fully "cured of the desire to do so again." But she was incurable. She had been a witness to the fact that her own father's brains had been blown out by the discharge of a heavily loaded gun, deliberately aimed at his head by his drunken master. She only needed half a chance to make still greater struggles than ever for freedom.

She had great faith in God, and found much solace in singing some of the good old Methodist tunes by day and night. Her owner, observing this apparently tranquil state of mind, indicating that she "seemed better contented than ever," concluded that it was safe to let the garret door remain unlocked at night. Not many weeks were allowed to pass before she resolved to again make a bold strike for freedom. This time she had to leave the two little boys, Levin and Peter, behind.

On the night she started, she went to the bed where they were sleeping, kissed them, and, consigning them into the hands of God, bade her mother good-bye, and with her two little girls wended her way again to Burlington County, New Jersey, but to a different neighborhood from that where she had been seized. She changed her name to Charity, and succeeded in again joining her husband, but, alas, with the heart-breaking thought that she had been compelled to leave her two little boys in slavery and one of the little girls on the road for the father to go back after. Thus she began life in freedom anew.

Levin and Peter, eight and six years of age respectively, were now left at the mercy of the enraged owner, and were soon hurried off to a Southern market and sold, while their mother, for whom they were daily weeping, was they knew not where. They were too young to know that they were slaves, or to understand the nature of the afflicting separation. Sixteen years before Peter's return, his older brother (Levin) died a slave in the State of Alabama, and was buried by his surviving brother, Peter.

No idea other than that they had been "kidnapped" from their mother ever entered their minds; nor had they any knowledge of the State from whence they supposed they had been taken, the last names of their mother and father, or where they were born. On the other hand, the mother was aware that the safety of herself and her rescued children depended on keeping the whole transaction a strict family secret. During the forty years of separation, except two or three Quaker friends, including the devoted friend of the slave, Benjamin Lundy, it is doubtful whether any other individuals were let into the secret of her slave life. And when the account given of Peter's return, etc., was published in 1850, it led some of the family to apprehend serious danger from the partial revelation of the early condition of the mother, especially as it was about the time that the Fugitive Slave law was passed.

Hence, the author of *The Kidnapped and the Ransomed* was compelled to omit these dangerous facts, and had to confine herself strictly to the "personal recollections of Peter Still" with regard to his being "kidnapped." Likewise, in the sketch of Seth Concklin's eventful life, written by Dr. W. H. Furness, for similar reasons he felt obliged to make but bare reference to his wonderful agency in relation to Peter's family, although he was fully aware of all the facts in the case.

Peter Still. The *Underground Railroad Records*, 1886.

Charity Still. The *Underground Railroad Records*, 1886.

Pages 86 – 97 from *Underground Rail Road Records*, 1886.

TRIAL OF THE EMANCIPATORS OF COL. J. H. WHEELER'S SLAVES: JANE JOHNSON AND HER TWO LITTLE BOYS

Among other duties devolving on the Vigilance Committee when hearing of slaves brought into the State by their owners, was immediately to inform such persons that as they were not fugitives, but were brought into the State by their masters, they were entitled to their freedom without another moment's service, and that they could have the assistance of the Committee and the advice of counsel without charge, by simply availing themselves of these proffered favors.

Many slave-holders fully understood the law in this particular, and were also equally posted with regard to the vigilance of abolitionists. Consequently they avoided bringing slaves beyond Mason and Dixon's Line in traveling North. But some slave-holders were not thus mindful of the laws, or were too arrogant to take heed, as may be seen in the case of Colonel John H. Wheeler, of North Carolina, the United States Minister to Nicaragua. In passing through Philadelphia from Washington one very warm July day in 1855, accompanied by three of his slaves, his high official equilibrium, as well as his assumed rights under the Constitution, received a terrible shock at the hands of the Committee. Therefore, for the readers of these pages, and in order to completely illustrate the various phases of the work of the Committee in the days

137

of Slavery, this case, selected from many others, is a fitting one. However, for more than a brief recital of some of the more prominent incidents, it will not be possible to find room in this volume. And, indeed, the necessity of so doing is precluded by the fact that Mr. Williamson, in justice to himself and the cause of freedom, with great pains and singular ability, gathered the most important facts bearing on his memorable trial and imprisonment, and published them in a neat volume for historical reference.

In order to bring fully before the reader the beginning of this interesting and exciting case, it seems only necessary to publish the subjoined letter, written by one of the actors in the drama, and addressed to the New York *Tribune*, and an additional paragraph which may be requisite to throw light on a special point, which Judge Kane decided was concealed in the "obstinate" breast of Passmore Williamson, as said Williamson persistently refused before the said Judge's court, to own that he had a knowledge of the mystery in question. After which, a brief glance at some of the more important points of the case must suffice.

LETTER COPIED FROM THE NEW YORK *TRIBUNE.*
[Correspondence of The N. Y. *Tribune.*]
PHILADELPHIA, Monday, July 30, 1855
As the public have not been made acquainted with the facts and particulars respecting the agency of Mr. Passmore Williamson and others, in relation to the slave case now agitating this city, and especially as the poor slave mother and her two sons have been so grossly misrepresented, I deem it my duty to lay the facts before you, for publication or otherwise, as you may think proper.

On Wednesday afternoon, week, at 4½ o'clock, the following note was placed in my hands by a colored boy whom I had never before seen, to my recollection:

"Mr. Still—Sir: Will you come down to Bloodgood's Hotel as soon as possible—as there are three fugitive slaves here and they want liberty. Their master is here with them, on his way to New York."

The note was without date, and the signature so indistinctly written as not to be understood by me, having evidently been penned in a moment of haste.

Without delay, I ran with the note to Mr. P. Williamson's office, Seventh and Arch, found him at his desk, and gave it to him, and after reading it, he remarked that he could not go down, as he had to go to Harrisburg that night on business—but he advised me to go, and to get the names of the slave-holder and the slaves, in order to telegraph to New York to have them arrested there, as no time remained to procure a writ of habeas corpus here.

I could not have been two minutes in Mr. W.'s office before starting in haste for the wharf. To my surprise, however, when I reached the wharf, there I found Mr. W., his mind having undergone a sudden change; he was soon on the spot.

I saw three or four colored persons in the hall at Bloodgood's, none of whom I recognized except the boy who brought me the note. Before having time for making inquiry, some one said they had gone on board the boat. "Get their description," said Mr. W. I instantly inquired of one of the colored persons for the desired description, and was told that she was "a tall, dark woman, with two little boys."

Mr. W. and myself ran on board of the boat, looked among the passengers on the first deck, but saw them not. "They are up on the second deck," an unknown voice uttered. In a second we were in their presence. We approached the anxious-looking slave-mother with her two boys on her left-hand; close on her right sat an ill-favored white man having a cane in his hand which I took to be a sword-cane. (As to its being a sword-cane, however, I might have been mistaken.)

The first words to the mother were: "Are you traveling?" "Yes," was the prompt answer. "With whom?" She nodded her head toward the ill-favored man, signifying with him. Fidgeting on his seat, he said something, exactly what I do not now recollect. In reply I remarked: "Do they belong to you, Sir?" "Yes, they are in my charge," was his answer. Turning from him to the mother and her sons, in substance, and word for word, as near as I can remember, the following remarks were earnestly though calmly addressed by the individuals who rejoiced to meet them on free soil, and who felt unmistakably assured that they were justified by the laws of Pennsylvania as well as the Law of God, in informing them of their rights:

"You are entitled to your freedom according to the laws of Pennsylvania, having been brought into the State by your owner. If you prefer freedom to slavery, as we suppose everybody does, you have the chance to accept it now. Act calmly—don't be frightened by your master—you are as much entitled to your freedom as we are, or as he is—be determined and you need have no fears but that you will be protected by the law. Judges have time and again decided cases in this city and State similar to yours in favor of freedom! Of course, if you want to remain a slave with your master, we cannot force you to leave; we only want to make you sensible of your rights. *Remember, if you lose this chance you may never get such another,*" etc.

This advice to the woman was made in the hearing of a number of persons present, white and colored; and one elderly white gentleman of genteel address, who seemed to take much interest in what was going on, remarked that they would have the same chance for their freedom in New Jersey and New York as they then had—seeming to sympathize with the woman, etc.

During the few moments in which the above remarks were made, the slave holder frequently interrupted—said she understood all about the laws making her free, and her right to leave if she wanted to; but contended that she did not want to leave—that she was on a visit to New York to see her friends—"afterward *wished to return to her three children whom she left in Virginia, from whom it would be* HARD *to separate her.* Furthermore, he diligently tried to constrain her to say that she did not want to be interfered with—that she wanted to go with him—that she was on a visit to New York—had children in the South, etc.; but the woman's desire to be free was altogether too strong to allow her to make a single acknowledgment favorable to his wishes in the matter. On the contrary, she repeatedly said, distinctly and firmly, "*I am not free, but I want my freedom* ALWAYS *wanted to be free!! but he holds me.*"

While the slaveholder claimed that she belonged to him, he said *that she was free!* Again he said that he was *going to give her her freedom*, etc. When his eyes would be off of hers, such eagerness as her looks expressed, indicative of her entreaty that we would not forsake her and her little ones in their weakness, it had never been my lot to witness before, under any circumstances.

The last bell tolled! The last moment for further delay passed! The arm of the woman being slightly touched, accompanied with the word, "Come!" she instantly arose. "Go along—go along!" said some, who sympathized, to the boys, at the same time taking hold of their arms. By this time the parties were fairly moving toward the stairway leading to

141

the deck below. Instantly on their starting, the slave-holder rushed at the woman and her children, to prevent their leaving; and, if I am not mistaken, he simultaneously took hold of the woman and Mr. Williamson, which resistance on his part caused Mr. W. to take hold of him and set him aside quickly.

The passengers were looking on all around, but none interfered in behalf of the slaveholder except one man, whom I took to be another slaveholder. He said harshly, "Let them alone; they are his *property!*" The youngest boy, about 7 years of age—too young to know what these things meant—cried "Massa John! Massa John!" The elder boy, 11 years of age, took the matter more dispassionately, and the mother quite calmly. The mother and her sympathizers all moved down the stairs together in the presence of quite a number of spectators on the first deck and on the wharf, all of whom, as far as I was able to discern, seemed to look upon the whole affair with the greatest indifference. The woman and children were assisted, but not forced to leave. Nor were there any violence or threatenings as I saw or heard. The only words that I heard from any one of an objectionable character, were: "Knock him down; knock him down!" but who uttered it or who was meant I knew not, nor have I since been informed. However, if it was uttered by a colored man, I regret it, as there was not the slightest cause for such language, especially as the sympathies of the spectators and citizens seemed to justify the course pursued.

While passing off of the wharf and down Delaware Avenue to Dock St., and up Dock to Front, where a carriage was procured, the slaveholder and one police officer were of the party, if no more.

The youngest boy on being put in the carriage was told that he was "a fool for crying so after 'Massa John,' who would sell him if he ever caught him." Not another whine was heard on the subject.

The carriage drove down town slowly, the horses being fatigued and the weather intensely hot; the inmates were put out on Tenth street—not at any house—after which they soon found hospitable friends and quietude. The excitement of the moment having passed by, the mother *seemed very cheerful, and rejoiced greatly that herself and boys had been, as she thought, so "providentially delivered from the house of bondage!"* For the first time in her life she could look upon herself and children and feel free!

Having felt the iron in her heart for the best half of her days—having been sold with her children on the auction block—having had one of her children sold far away from her without hope of her seeing him again—she very naturally and wisely concluded to go to Canada, fearing if she remained in this city—as some assured her she could do with entire safety—that she might again find herself in the clutches of the tyrant from whom she had fled.

A few items of what she related concerning the character of her master may be interesting to the reader—

Within the last two years he had sold all his slaves— between thirty and forty in number—having purchased the present ones in that space of time. She said that before leaving Washington, coming on the cars, and at his father-in-law's in this city, a number of persons had told him that in bringing his slaves into Pennsylvania they would be free. When told at his father-in-law's, as she overheard it, that he "could not have done a worse thing," &c., he replied that "Jane would not leave him."

As much, however, as he affected to have such implicit confidence in Jane, he scarcely allowed her to be out of his presence a moment while in this city. To use Jane's own language, he was "on her heels every minute," fearing that some one might get to her ears the sweet music of freedom. By the way, Jane had it deep in her heart before leaving the South, and was bent on succeeding in New York, if disappointed in Philadelphia.

At Bloodgood's, after having been belated and left by the 2 o'clock train, while waiting for the 5 o'clock line, his appetite tempted her "master" to take a hasty dinner. So after placing Jane where he thought she would be pretty secure from "evil communications" from the colored waiters, and after giving her a double counselling, he made his way to the table; remained but a little while, however, before leaving to look after Jane; finding her composed, looking over a bannister near where he left her, he returned to the table again and finished his meal.

But, alas, for the slave-holder! Jane had her "top eye open," and in that brief space had appealed to the sympathies of a person whom she ventured to trust, saying, "I and my children are slaves, and we want liberty!" I am not certain, but suppose that person, in the goodness of his heart, was the cause of the note being sent to the Anti-Slavery office, and hence the result.

As to her going on to New York to see her friends, and wishing to return to her three children in the South, and his going to free her, etc., Jane declared repeatedly and very positively, that there was not a particle of truth in what her master said on these points. The truth is she had not the slightest hope of freedom through any act of his. She had only left one boy in the South, who had been sold far away, where she scarcely ever heard from him, indeed never expected to see him any more.

In appearance Jane is tall and well formed, high and large forehead, of genteel manners, chestnut color, and seems to possess, naturally, uncommon good sense, though of course she has never been allowed to read.

Thus I have given as truthful a report as I am capable of doing, of Jane and the circumstances connected with her deliverance.

W. Still

P. S.—Of the five colored porters who promptly appeared, with warm hearts throbbing in sympathy with the mother and her children, too much cannot be said in commendation. In the present case they acted nobly, whatever may be said of their general character, of which I know nothing. How human beings, who have ever tasted oppression, could have acted differently under the circumstances I cannot conceive.

Rescue of Jane Johnson and her children. The *Underground Railroad Records*, 1886.

The mystery alluded to, which the above letter did not contain, and which the court failed to make Mr. Williamson reveal, might have been truthfully explained in these words. The carriage was procured at the wharf, while Col. Wheeler and Mr. Williamson were debating the question relative to the action of the Committee, and at that instant, Jane and her two boys were invited into it, and accompanied by the writer, who procured it, were driven down town, and on Tenth Street, below Lombard, the inmates were invited out of it, and the said conductor paid the driver and discharged him. For prudential reasons he took them to a temporary resting-place, where they could tarry until after dark; then they were invited to his own residence, where they were made welcome, and in due time forwarded East. Now, what disposition was made of them after they had left the wharf, while Williamson and Wheeler were discussing matters— (as was clearly sworn to by Passmore, in his answer to the writ of Habeas Corpus)—he, Williamson, did not know. That evening, before seeing the member of the Committee, with whom he acted in concert on the boat, and who had entire charge of Jane and her boys, he left for Harrisburg, to fulfill business engagements. The next morning his father (Thomas Williamson) brought the writ of Habeas Corpus (which had been served at Passmore's office after he left) to the Anti-Slavery Office. In his calm manner, he handed it to the writer, at the same time remarking that "Passmore had gone to Harrisburg," and added, "thee had better attend to it" (the writ). Edward Hopper, Esq., was applied to with the writ, and in the absence of Mr.

Williamson, appeared before the court, and stated "that the writ had not been served, as Mr. W. was out of town," etc.

After this statement, the Judge postponed further action until the next day. In the meanwhile, Mr. Williamson returned and found the writ awaiting him, and an agitated state of feeling throughout the city besides. Now it is very certain, that he did not seek to know from those in the secret, where Jane Johnson and her boys were taken after they left the wharf, or as to what disposition had been made of them, in any way; except to ask simply, "are they safe?" (and when told "yes," he smiled). Consequently, he might have been examined for a week, by the most skillful lawyer at the Philadelphia bar, but he could not have answered other than he did in making his return to the writ before Judge Kane, namely: "*That the persons named in the writ, nor either of them, are now nor was at the time of issuing of the writ, or the original writ, or at any other time in the custody, power, or possession of the respondent, nor by him confined or restrained; wherefore he cannot have the bodies,*" etc.

Thus, while Mr. W. was subjected to the severest trial of his devotion to Freedom, his noble bearing throughout, won for him the admiration and sympathy of the friends of humanity and liberty throughout the entire land, and in proof of his fidelity, he most cheerfully submitted to imprisonment rather than desert his principles. But the truth was not wanted in this instance by the enemies of Freedom; obedience to Slavery was demanded to satisfy the South. The opportunity seemed favorable for teaching abolitionists and negroes, that they had no right to interfere with a "chivalrous southern gentleman," while passing through Philadelphia with his slaves. Thus, to make an effective blow, all the pro-slavery elements of Philadelphia were brought into action, and matters looked for a time as though Slavery in this instance would have everything its own way. Passmore was locked up in prison on the flimsy pretext of contempt of court, and true bills were found against him and half a dozen colored men, charging them with "riot," "forcible abduction," and "assault and battery," and there was no lack of hard swearing on the part of Col. Wheeler and his proslavery sympathizers in substantiation of these grave charges. But the pro-slaveryites had counted without their host—Passmore would not yield an inch, but stood as firmly by his principles in prison, as he did on the boat. Indeed, it was soon evident, that his resolute course was bringing floods of sympathy from the ablest and best minds throughout the North. On the other hand, the occasion was rapidly awakening thousands daily, who had hitherto manifested little or no interest at all on the subject, to the wrongs of the slave.

It was soon discovered by the "chivalry" that keeping Mr. Williamson in prison would indirectly greatly aid the cause of Freedom—that every day he remained would make numerous converts to the cause of liberty; that Mr. Williamson was doing ten-fold more in prison for the cause of universal liberty than he could possibly do while pursuing his ordinary vocation.

With regard to the colored men under bonds, Col. Wheeler and his satellites felt very confident that there was no room for them to escape. They must have had reason so to think, judging from the hard swearing they did, before the committing magistrate. Consequently, in the order of events, while Passmore was still in prison, receiving visits from hosts of friends, and letters of sympathy from all parts of the North, William Still, William Curtis, James P. Braddock, John Ballard, James Martin and Isaiah Moore, were brought into court for trial. The first name on the list in the proceedings of the court was called up first.

Against this individual, it was pretty well understood by the friends of the slave, that no lack of pains and false swearing would be resorted to on the part of Wheeler and his witnesses to gain a verdict.

Mr. McKim and other noted abolitionists managing the defense were equally alive to the importance of over-whelming the enemy in this particular issue. The Hon. Charles Gibbons was engaged to defend William Still, and William S. Peirce, Esq., and William B. Birney, Esq., the other five colored defendants.

In order to make the victory complete, the anti-slavery friends deemed it of the highest importance to have Jane Johnson in court, to face her master, and under oath to sweep away his "refuge of lies," with regard to her being "abducted," and her unwillingness to "leave her master," etc. So Mr. McKim and the friends very privately arranged to have Jane Johnson on hand at the opening of the defense.

Mrs. Lucretia Mott, Mrs. McKim, Miss Sarah Pugh and Mrs. Plumly volunteered to accompany this poor slave mother to the court-house and to occupy seats by her side, while she should face her master, and boldly, on oath, contradict all his hard swearing. A better subject for the occasion than Jane could not have been desired. She entered the court room veiled, and of course was not known by the crowd, as pains had been taken to keep the public in ignorance of the fact that she was to be brought on to bear witness. So that, at the conclusion of the second witness on the part of the defense, "Jane Johnson" was called for, in a shrill voice. Deliberately, Jane arose and answered in a lady-like manner to her name, and was then the observed of all observers. Never before had such a scene been witnessed in Philadelphia. It was indescribable. Substantially, her testimony on this occasion was in keeping with the subjoined affidavit, which was as follows—

"*State of New York, City and County of New York.*

"Jane Johnson being sworn, makes oath and says—

"My name is Jane—Jane Johnson; I was the slave of Mr. Wheeler of Washington; he bought me and my two children, about two years ago, of Mr. Cornelius Crew, of Richmond, Va.; my youngest child is between six and seven years old, the other between ten and eleven; I have one other child only, and he is in Richmond; I have not seen him for about two years; never expect to see him again; Mr. Wheeler brought me and my two children to Philadelphia, on the way to Nicaragua, to wait on his wife; I didn't want to go without my two children, and he consented to take them; we came to Philadelphia by the cars; stopped at Mr. Sully's, Mr. Wheeler's father-in-law, a few moments; then went to the steamboat for New York at 2 o'clock, but were too late; we went into Bloodgood's

Hotel; Mr. Wheeler went to dinner; Mr. Wheeler had told me in Washington to have nothing to say to colored persons, and if any of them spoke to me, to say I was a free woman traveling with a minister; we staid at Bloodgood's till 5 o'clock; Mr. Wheeler kept his eye on me all the time except when he was at dinner; he left his dinner to come and see if I was safe, and then went back again; while he was at dinner, I saw a colored woman and told her I was a slave woman, that my master had told me not to speak to colored people, and that if any of them spoke to me to say that I was free; but I am not free; but I want to be free; she said: 'poor thing, I pity you'; after that I saw a colored man and said the same thing to him, he said he would telegraph to New York, and two men would meet me at 9 o'clock and take me with them; after that we went on board the boat, Mr. Wheeler sat beside me on the deck; I saw a colored gentleman come on board, he beckoned to me; I nodded my head, and could not go; Mr. Wheeler was beside me and I was afraid; a white gentleman then came and said to Mr. Wheeler, 'I want to speak to your servant, and tell her of her rights'; Mr. Wheeler rose and said, 'If you have anything to say, say it to me—she knows her rights'; the white gentleman asked me if I wanted to be free; I said 'I do, but I belong to this gentleman and I can't have it'; he replied, 'Yes, you can, come with us, you are as free as your master, if you want your freedom come now; if you go back to Washington you may never get it'; I rose to go. Mr. Wheeler spoke, and said, 'I will give you your freedom,' but he had never promised it before, and I knew he would never give it to me; the white gentleman held out his hand and I went toward him; I was ready for the word before it was given me; I took the children by the hands, who both cried, for they were frightened, but both stopped when they got on shore; a colored man carried the little one, I led the other by the hand. We walked down the street till we got to a hack; nobody forced me away; nobody pulled me, and nobody led me; I went away of my own free will; I always wished to be free and meant to be free when I came North; I hardly expected it in Philadelphia, but I thought I should get free in New York; I have been comfortable and happy since I left Mr. Wheeler, and so are the children; I don't want to go back; I could have gone in Philadelphia if I had wanted to; I could go now; but I had rather die than go back. I wish to make this statement before a magistrate, because I understand that Mr. Williamson is in prison on my account, and I hope the truth may be of benefit to him."

her
Jane ✕ Johnson.
mark.

It might have been supposed that her honest and straightforward testimony would have been sufficient to cause even the most relentless slaveholder to abandon at once a pursuit so monstrous and utterly hopeless as Wheeler's was. But although he was sadly confused and put to shame, he hung on to the "lost cause" tenaciously. And his counsel, David Webster, Esq., and the United States District Attorney, Vandyke, completely imbued with the pro-slavery spirit, were equally as unyielding. And thus, with a zeal befitting the most worthy object imaginable, they labored with untiring effort to convict the colored men.

By this policy, however, the counsel for the defense was doubly aroused. Mr. Gibbons, in the most eloquent and indignant strains, perfectly annihilated the "distinguished Colonel John H. Wheeler, United States Minister Plenipotentiary near the Island of Nicaragua," taking special pains to ring the changes repeatedly on his long appellations. Mr. Gibbons appeared to be precisely in the right mood to make himself surpassingly forcible and eloquent on whatever point of law he chose to touch bearing on the case; or in whatever direction he chose to glance at the injustice and cruelty of the South. Most vividly did he draw the contrast between the States of "Georgia" and "Pennsylvania," with regard to the atrocious laws of Georgia. Scarcely less vivid is the impression, after a lapse of sixteen years, than when this eloquent speech was made. With the District Attorney, Wm. B. Mann, Esq., and his Honor, Judge Kelley, the defendants had no cause to complain. Throughout the entire proceedings, they had reason to feel that neither of these officials sympathized in the least with Wheeler or Slavery. Indeed, in the Judge's charge, and also in the District Attorney's closing speech, the ring of freedom could be distinctly heard—much more so than was agreeable to Wheeler and his Pro-Slavery sympathizers. The case of Wm. Still ended in his acquittal; the other five colored men were taken up in order. And it is scarcely necessary to say that Messrs. Peirce and Birney did full justice to all concerned. Mr. Peirce, especially, was one of the oldest, ablest and most faithful lawyers to the slave of the Philadelphia Bar. He never was known, it may safely be said, to hesitate in the darkest days of

Jane Johnson. The *Underground Rail Road Records*, 1886.

Passmore Williamson. Philadelphia: E. H. Coggins, Engraver & Printer, [1855?]. Marian S. Carson collection, Library of Congress.

Slavery to give his time and talents to the fugitive, even in the most hopeless cases, and when, from the unpopularity of such a course, serious sacrifices would be likely to result. Consequently, he was but at home in this case, and most nobly did he defend his clients, with the same earnestness that a man would defend his fireside against the approach of burglars. At the conclusion of the trial, the jury returned a verdict of "not guilty," as to all the persons in the first count, charging them with riot. In the second count, charging them with "Assault and Battery" (on Col. Wheeler), Ballard and Curtis were found "guilty," the rest "not guilty." The guilty were given about a week in jail. Thus ended this act in the Wheeler drama.

The following extract is taken from the correspondence of the New York *Tribune* touching Jane Johnson's presence in the court, and will be interesting on that account:

"But it was a bold and perilous move on the part of her friends, and the deepest apprehensions were felt for a while, for the result. The United States Marshal was there with his warrant and an extra force to execute it. The officers of the court and other State officers were there to protect the witness and vindicate the laws of the State. Vandyke, the United States District Attorney, swore he would take her. The State officers swore he should not, and for a while it seemed that nothing could avert a bloody scene. It was expected that the conflict would take place at the door, when she should leave the room, so that when she and her friends went out, and for some time after, the most intense suspense pervaded the courtroom. She was, however, allowed to enter the carriage that awaited her without disturbance. She was accompanied by Mr. McKim, Secretary of the Pennsylvania Anti-Slavery Society, Lucretia Mott and George Corson, one of our most manly and intrepid police officers. The carriage was followed by another filled with officers as a guard; and thus escorted she was taken back in safety to the house from which she had been brought. Her title to Freedom under the laws of the State will hardly again be brought into question."

Mr. Williamson was committed to prison by Judge Kane for contempt of Court, on the 27th day of July, 1855, and was released on the 3d day of November the same year, having gained, in the estimation of the friends of Freedom every where, a triumph and a fame which but few men in the great moral battle for Freedom could claim.

Pages 348 – 68 from *Underground Rail Road Records*, 1886

THE SLAVE-HUNTING TRAGEDY IN LANCASTER COUNTY, IN SEPTEMBER, 1851
"Treason at Christiana"

Having inserted the Fugitive Slave Bill in these records of the Underground Rail Road [in the complete edition], one or two slave cases will doubtless suffice to illustrate the effect of its passage on the public mind, and the colored people in particular. The deepest feelings of loathing, contempt and opposition were manifested by the opponents of Slavery on every hand. Antislavery papers, lecturers, preachers, etc., arrayed themselves boldly against it on the ground of its inhumanity and violation of the laws of God.

On the other hand, the slaveholders of the South, and their pro-slavery adherents in the North demanded the most abject obedience from all parties, regardless of conscience or obligation to God. In order to compel such obedience, as well as to prove the practicability of the law, unbounded zeal daily marked the attempt on the part of slave-holders and slave-catchers to refasten the fetters on the limbs of fugitives in different parts of the North, whither they had escaped.

In this dark hour, when colored men's rights were so insecure, as a matter of self-defence, they felt allied upon to arm themselves and resist all kidnapping intruders, although clothed with the authority of wicked law. Among the most exciting cases tending to justify this course, the following may be named:

JAMES HAMLET was the first slave case who was summarily arrested under the Fugitive Slave Law, and sent back to bondage from New York.

WILLIAM and ELLEN CRAFT were hotly pursued to Boston by hunters from Georgia.

ADAM GIBSON, a free colored man, residing in Philadelphia, was arrested, delivered into the hands of his alleged claimants, by commissioner Edward D. Ingraham, and hurried into Slavery.

EUPHEMIA WILLIAMS (the mother of six living children),—her case excited much interest and sympathy.

SHADRACH was arrested and rescued in Boston.

HANNAH DELLUM and her child were returned to Slavery from Philadelphia.

THOMAS HALL and his wife were pounced upon at midnight in Chester county, beaten and dragged off to Slavery, etc.

And, as if gloating over their repeated successes, and utterly regardless of all caution, about one year after the passage of this nefarious bill, a party of slave-hunters arranged for a grand capture at Christiana.

One year from the passage of the law, at a time when alarm and excitement were running high, the most decided stand was taken at Christiana, in the State of Pennsylvania, to defeat the law, and defend freedom. Fortunately for the fugitives, the plans of the slave-hunters and officials leaked out while arrangements were making in Philadelphia for the capture, and, information being sent to the anti-slavery office, a messenger was at once dispatched to Christiana to put all persons supposed to be in danger on their guard.

Among those thus notified were brave hearts, who did not believe in running away from slave-catchers. They resolved to stand up for the right of self-defence. They loved liberty and hated Slavery, and when the slave-catchers arrived, they were prepared for them. Of the contest, on that bloody morning, we have copied a report, carefully written at the time, by C. C. Burleigh, editor of the *Pennsylvania Freeman*, who visited the scene of battle, immediately after it was over, and doubtless obtained as faithful an account of all the facts in the case, as could then be had.

"Last Thursday morning (the 11th inst.), a peaceful neighborhood in the borders of Lancaster county was made the scene of a bloody battle, resulting from an attempt to capture seven colored men as fugitive slaves. As the reports of the affray which came to us were contradictory, and having good reason to believe that those of the daily press were grossly one-sided and unfair, we repaired to the scene of the tragedy, and, by patient inquiry and careful examination, endeavored to learn the real facts. To do this, from the varying and conflicting statements which we encountered, scarcely two of which agreed in every point, was not easy; but we believe the account we give below, as the result of these inquiries, is substantially correct.

Very early on the 11th inst., a party of slave-hunters went into a neighborhood about two miles west of Christiana, near the eastern border of Lancaster county, in pursuit of fugitive slaves. The party consisted of Edward Gorsuch, his son, Dickerson Gorsuch, his nephew, Dr. Pearce, Nicholas Hutchins, and others, all from Baltimore county,

Md., and one Henry H. Kline, a notorious slave-catching constable from Philadelphia, who had been deputized by Commissioner Ingraham for this business. At about day-dawn they were discovered lying in an ambush near the house of one William Parker, a colored man, by an inmate of the house, who had started for his work. He fled back to the house, pursued by the slave-hunters, who entered the lower part of the house, but were unable to force their way into the upper part, to which the family had retired. A horn was blown from an upper window; two shots were fired, both, as we believe, though we are not certain, by the assailants, one at the colored man who fled into the house, and the other at the inmates, through the window. No one was wounded by either. A parley ensued. The slave-holder demanded his slaves, who he said were concealed in the house. The colored men presented themselves successively at the window, and asked if they were the slaves claimed; Gorsuch said that neither of them was his slave. They told him that they were the only colored men in the house, and were determined never to be taken alive as slaves. Soon the colored people of the neighborhood, alarmed by the horn, began to gather, armed with guns, axes, corn-cutters, or clubs. Mutual threatenings were uttered by the two parties. The slave-holders told the blacks that resistance would be useless, as they had a party of thirty men in the woods near by. The blacks warned them again to leave, as they would die before they would go into Slavery.

From an hour to an hour and a half passed in these parleyings, angry conversations, and threats; the blacks increasing by new arrivals, until they probably numbered from thirty to fifty, most of them armed in some way. About this time, Castner Hanaway, a white man, and a Friend, who resided in the neighborhood, rode up, and was soon followed by Elijah Lewis, another Friend, a merchant, in Cooperville, both gentlemen highly esteemed as worthy and peaceable citizens. As they came up, Kline, the deputy marshal, ordered them to aid him, as a United States officer, to capture the fugitive slaves. They refused of course, as would any man not utterly destitute of honor, humanity, and moral principle, and warned the assailants that it was madness for them to attempt to capture fugitive slaves there, or even to remain, and begged them if they wished to save their own lives, to leave the ground. Kline replied, "Do you really think so?" " Yes," was the answer, "the sooner you leave, the better, if you would prevent bloodshed." Kline then left the ground, retiring into a very safe distance into a cornfield, and toward the woods. The blacks were so exasperated by his threats that, but for the interposition of the two white Friends, it is very doubtful whether he would have escaped without injury. Messrs. Hanaway and Lewis both exerted their influence to dissuade the colored people from violence, and would probably have succeeded in restraining them, had not the assailing party fired upon them. Young Gorsuch asked his father to leave, but the old man refused, declaring, as it is said and believed, that he would "go to hell, or have his slaves."

Finding they could do nothing further, Hanaway and Lewis both started to leave, again counselling the slave-hunters to go away, and the colored people to peace, but had gone but a few rods, when one of the inmates of the house attempted to come out at the door. Gorsuch presented his revolver, ordering him back. The colored man replied, " You had better go away, if you don't want to get hurt," and at the same time pushed him aside and passed out. Maddened at this, and stimulated by the question of his nephew, whether he would "take such an insult from a d—d nigger," Gorsuch fired at the colored man, and was followed by his son and nephew, who both fired their revolvers. The fire was returned by the blacks, who made a rush upon them at the same time. Gorsuch and his son fell, the one dead the other wounded. The rest of the party after firing their revolvers, fled precipitately through the corn and to the woods, pursued by some of the blacks. One was wounded, the rest escaped unhurt. Kline, the deputy marshal, who now boasts of his miraculous escape from a volley of musketballs, had kept at a safe distance, though urged by young Gorsuch to stand by his father and protect him, when he refused to leave the ground. He of course came off unscathed. Several colored men were wounded, but none severely. Some had their hats or their clothes perforated with bullets; others had flesh wounds. They said that the Lord protected them, and they shook the bullets from their clothes. One man found several shot in his boot, which seemed to have spent their force before reaching him, and did not even break the skin. The slave-holders having fled, several neighbors, mostly Friends and anti-slavery men, gathered to succor the wounded and take charge of the dead. "We are told that Parker himself protected the wounded man from his excited comrades, and brought water and a bed from his own house for the invalid, thus showing that he was as magnanimous to his fallen enemy as he was brave in the defence of his own liberty. The young man was then removed to a neighboring house, where the family received him with the tenderest kindness and paid him every attention, though they told him in Quaker phrase, that "they had no unity with his cruel business," and were very sorry to see him engaged in it. He was much affected by their kindness, and we are told, expressed his regret that he had been thus engaged, and his determination, if his life was spared, never again to make a similar attempt. His wounds are very severe, and it is feared mortal. All attempts to procure assistance to capture the fugitive slaves failed, the people in the neighborhood either not relishing the business of slave-catching, or at least, not choosing to risk their lives in it. There was a very great reluctance felt to going even to remove the body and the wounded man, until several abolitionists and Friends had collected for that object, when others found courage to follow on. The excitement caused by this most melancholy affair is very great among all classes. The abolitionists, of course, mourn the occurrence, while they see in it a legitimate fruit of the Fugitive Slave Law, just such a harvest of blood as they had long feared that the law would produce, and which they had earnestly labored to prevent. We believe that they alone, of all classes of the nation, are free from responsibility for its occurrence, having wisely foreseen the danger, and faithfully labored to avert it by removing its causes, and preventing the inhuman policy which has hurried on the bloody convulsion.

The Christiana Tragedy. The *Underground Rail Road Records*, 1886.

The enemies of the colored people are making this the occasion of fresh injuries, and a more bitter ferocity toward that defenceless people, and of new misrepresentation and calumnies against the abolitionists.

The colored people, though the great body of them had no connection with this affair, are hunted like partridges upon the mountains, by the relentless horde, which has been poured forth upon them under the pretense of arresting the parties concerned in the fight. "When we reached Christiana, on Friday afternoon, we found that the Deputy-Attorney Thompson, of Lancaster, was there, and had issued warrants, upon the depositions of Kline and others, for the arrest of all suspected persons. A company of police were scouring the neighborhood in search of colored people, several of whom were seized while at their work near by, and brought in.

CASTNER HANAWAY and ELIJAH LEWIS, hearing that warrants were issued against them, came to Christiana, and voluntarily gave themselves up, calm and strong in the confidence of their innocence. They, together with the arrested colored men, were sent to Lancaster jail that night.

The next morning we visited the ground of the battle, and the family where young Gorsuch now lives, and while there, we saw a deposition which he had just made, that he believed no white persons were engaged in the affray, beside his own party. As he was on the ground during the whole controversy, and deputy Marshall Kline had discreetly run off into the cornfield, before the fighting began, the hireling slave-catcher's eager and confident testimony against our white friends, will, we think, weigh lightly with impartial men.

On returning to Christiana, we found that the United States Marshal from the city had arrived at that place, accompanied by Commissioner Ingraham, Mr. Jones, a special commissioner of the United States from Washington, the U. S. District Attorney Ashmead, with forty-five U. S. Marines from the Navy Yard, and a posse of about forty of the City Marshal's police, together with a large body of special constables, eager for such a man hunt, from Columbia and Lancaster and other places. This crowd divided into parties, of from ten to twenty-five, and scoured the country, in every direction, for miles around, ransacking the houses of the colored people, and captured every colored man they could find, with several colored women, and two other white men. Never did our heart bleed with deeper pity

165

for the peeled and persecuted colored people than when we saw this troop let loose upon them, and witnessed the terror and distress which its approach excited in families, wholly innocent of the charges laid against them."

On the other hand, a few extracts from the editorials of some of the leading papers will suffice to show the state of public feeling at that time, and the dreadful opposition abolitionists and fugitives had to contend with. From one of the leading daily journals of Philadelphia, we copy as follows:

"There can be no difference of opinion concerning the shocking affair which occurred at Christiana, on Thursday, the resisting of a law of Congress by a band of armed negroes, whereby the majesty of the Government was defied and life taken in one and the same act. There is something more than a mere ordinary, something more than even a murderous, riot in all this. It is an act of insurrection, we might, considering the peculiar class and condition of the guilty parties, almost call it a servile insurrection—if not also one of treason. Fifty, eighty, or a hundred persons, whether white or black, who are deliberately in arms for the purpose of resisting the law, even the law for the recovery of fugitive slaves, are in the attitude of levying war against the United States; and doubly heavy becomes the crime of murder in such a case, and doubly serious the accountability of all who have any connection with the act as advisers, suggesters, countenancers, or accessories in any way whatever."

In those days, the paper from which this extract is taken represented the Whig party and the more moderate and respectable class of citizens.

The following is an extract from a leading democratic organ of Philadelphia:

"We will not, however, insult the reader by arguing that which has not been heretofore doubted, and which is not doubted now, by ten honest men in the State, and that is that the abolitionists are implicated in the Christiana murder. All the ascertained facts go to show that they were the real, if not the chief, instigators. White men are known to harbor fugitives in the neighborhood of Christiana, and these white men are known to be abolitionists, known to be opposed to the Fugitive Slave Law, and known to be the warm friends of William F. Johnston (Governor of the State of Pennsylvania). And, as if to clinch the argument, no less than three white men are now in the Lancaster prison, and were arrested as accomplices in the dreadful affair on the morning of the eleventh. And one of these white men was committed on a charge of high treason, on Saturday last, by United States Commissioner Ingraham."

Another daily paper of opposite politics thus spake:

"The unwarrantable outrage committed last week, at Christiana, Lancaster county, is a foul stain upon the fair name and fame of our State. We are pleased to see that the officers of the Federal and State Governments are upon the tracks of those who were engaged in the riot, and that several arrests have been made.

We do not wish to see the poor misled blacks who participated in the affair suffer to any great extent, for they were but tools. The men who are really chargeable with treason against the United States Government, and with the death of Mr. Gorsuch, an estimable citizen of Maryland, are unquestionably white, with hearts black enough to incite them to the commission of any crime equal in atrocity to that committed in Lancaster county. Pennsylvania has now but one course to pursue, and that is to aid, and warmly aid, the United States in bringing to condign punishment every man engaged in the riot. She owes it to herself and to the Union. Let her in this resolve be just and fearless."

From a leading neutral daily paper the following is taken: "One would suppose from the advice of forcible resistance, so familiarly given by the abolitionists, that they are quite unaware that there is any such crime as treason recognized by the Constitution, or punished with death by the laws of the United States. We would remind them that not only is there such a crime, but that there is a solemn decision of the Supreme Court that all who are concerned in a conspiracy which ripens into treason, whether present or absent from the scene of actual violence, are involved in the same liabilities as the immediate actors. If they engage in the conspiracy and stimulate the treason, they may keep their bodies from the affray without saving their necks from a halter.

It would be very much to the advantage of society if an example could be made of some of these persistent agitators, who excite the ignorant and reckless to treasonable violence, from which they themselves shrink, but who are, not only in morals, but in law, equally guilty and equally amenable to punishment with the victims of their inflammatory counsels."

A number of the most influential citizens represented the occurrence to the Governor as follows:

"To the Governor of Pennsylvania:

The undersigned, citizens of Pennsylvania, respectfully represent:

That citizens of a neighboring State have been cruelly assassinated by a band of armed outlaws at a place not more than three hours' journey distant from the seat of Government and from the commercial metropolis of the State:

That this insurrectionary movement in one of the most populous parts of the State has been so far successful as to overawe the local ministers of justice and paralyze the power of the law:

That your memorialists are not aware that 'any military force' has been sent to the seat of insurrection, or that the civil authority has been strengthened by the adoption of any measures suited to the momentous crisis.

They, therefore, respectfully request the chief executive magistrate of Pennsylvania to take into consideration the necessity of vindicating the outraged laws, and sustaining the dignity of the Commonwealth on this important and melancholy occasion."

Under this high pressure of public excitement, threatening and alarm breathed so freely on every hand that fugitive slaves and their friends in this region of Pennsylvania, at least, were compelled to pass through an hour of dreadful darkness—an ordeal extremely trying. The authorities of the United States, as well as the authorities of the State of Pennsylvania and Maryland, were diligently making arrests wherever a suspected party could be found, who happened to belong in the neighborhood of Christiana.

In a very short time the following persons were in custody: J. Castner Hanaway, Elijah Lewis, Joseph Scarlett, Samuel Kendig, Henry Spins, George Williams, Charles Hunter, Wilson Jones, Francis Harkins, Benjamin Thomson, William Brown (No. 1), William Brown (No. 2), John Halliday, Elizabeth Mosey, John Morgan, Joseph Berry, John Norton, Denis Smith, Harvey Scott, Susan Clark, Tansy Brown, Eliza Brown, Eliza Parker, Hannah Pinckney, Robert Johnson, Miller Thompson, Isaiah Clark, and Jonathan Black.

These were not all, but sufficed for a beginning; at least it made an interesting entertainment for the first day's examination; and although there were two or three non-resistant Quakers, and a number of poor defenceless colored women among those thus taken as prisoners, still it seemed utterly impossible for the exasperated defenders of Slavery to divest themselves of the idea that this heroic deed in self-defence, on the part of men who felt that their liberties were in danger, was anything less than actually levying war against the United States.

Accordingly, therefore, the hearing gravely took place at Lancaster. On the side of the Commonwealth, the following distinguished counsel appeared on examination: Hon. John L. Thompson, District Attorney; Wm. B. Faulney, Esq.; Thos. E. Franklin, Esq., Attorney-General of Lancaster county; George L. Ashmead, Esq., of Philadelphia, representative of the United States authorities; and Hon. Robert Brent, Attorney-General of Maryland.

For the defence—Hon. Thaddeus Stevens, Reah Frazer, Messrs. Ford, Cline, and Dickey, Esquires.

From a report of the first day's hearing we copy a short extract, as follows:

"The excitement at Christiana during yesterday was very great. Several hundred persons were present, and the deepest feeling was manifested against the perpetrators of the outrage. At two o'clock yesterday afternoon, the United States Marshal, Mr. Roberts, United States District Attorney, J. W. Ashmead, Esq., Mr. Commissioner Ingraham, and Recorder Lee, accompanied by the United States Marines, returned to the city. Lieut. Johnson, and officers Lewis S. Brest, Samuel Mitchell, Charles McCully, Samuel Neff, Jacob Albright, Robert McEwen, and— Perkenpine, by direction of the United States Marshal, had charge of the following named prisoners, who were safely lodged in Moyamensing prison, accompanied by the Marines:—Joseph Scarlett (white), William Brown, Ezekiel Thompson, Isaiah Clarkson, Daniel Caulsberry, Benjamin Pendergrass, Elijah Clark, George W. H. Scott, Miller Thompson, and Samuel Hanson, all colored. The last three were placed in the debtors' apartment, and the others in the criminal apartment of the Moyamensing prison to await their trial for treason, &c."

In alluding to the second day's doings, the *Philadelphia Ledger* thus represented matters at the field of battle:

"The intelligence received last evening represents the country for miles around to be in as much excitement as at any time since the horrible deed was committed. The officers sent there at the instance of the proper authorities are making diligent search in every direction, and securing every person against whom the least suspicion is attached. The police force from this city, amounting to about sixty men, are under the marshalship of Lieut. Ellis. Just as the cars started east in the afternoon, five more prisoners who were secured at a place called the Welsh Mountains, twelve miles distant, were brought into Christiana. They were placed in custody until such time as a hearing will take place."

Although the government had summoned its ablest legal talent and the popular sentiment was as a hundred to one against William Parker and his brave comrades who had made the slave-hunter "bite the dust," most nobly did Thaddeus Stevens prove that he was not to be cowed, that he believed in the stirring sentiment so much applauded by the American people, "Give me liberty, or give me death," not only for the white man but for all men. Thus standing upon such great and invulnerable principles, it was soon discovered that one could chase a thousand, and two put ten thousand to flight in latter as well as in former times.

At first even the friends of freedom thought that the killing of Gorsuch was not only wrong, but unfortunate for the cause. Scarcely a week passed, however, before the matter was looked upon in a far different light, and it was pretty generally thought that, if the Lord had not a direct hand in it, the cause of Freedom at least would be greatly benefited thereby.

And just in proportion as the masses cried Treason! Treason! the hosts of freedom from one end of the land to the other were awakened to sympathize with the slave.

Thousands were soon aroused to show sympathy who had hitherto been dormant. Hundreds visited the prisoners in their cells to greet, cheer, and offer them aid and counsel in their hour of sore trial.

The friends of freedom remained calm even while the pro-slavery party were fiercely raging and gloating over the prospect, as they evidently thought of the satisfaction to be derived from teaching the abolitionists a lesson from the scaffold, which would in future prevent Underground Rail Road passengers from killing their masters when in pursuit of them.

Through the efforts of the authorities three white men, and twenty-seven colored had been safely lodged in Moyamensing prison, under the charge of treason. The authorities, however, had utterly failed to catch the hero, William Parker, as he had been sent to Canada, via the Underground Rail Road, and was thus "sitting under his own vine and fig tree, where none dared to molest, or make him afraid."

As an act of simple justice, it may here be stated that the abolitionists and prisoners found a true friend and ally at least in one United States official, who, by the way, figured prominently in making arrests, etc., namely: the United States Marshal, A. E. Roberts. In all his intercourse with the prisoners and their friends, he plainly showed that all his sympathies were on the side of Freedom, and not with the popular pro-slavery sentiment which clamored so loudly against traitors and abolitionists.

Two of his prisoners had been identified in the jail as fugitive slaves by their owners. When the trial came on these two individuals were among the missing. How they escaped was unknown; the Marshal, however, was strongly suspected of being a friend of the Underground Rail Road, and to add now, that those suspicions were founded on fact, will, doubtless, do him no damage.

In order to draw the contrast between Freedom and Slavery, simply with a view of showing how the powers that were acted and judged in the days of the reign of the Fugitive Slave Law, unquestionably nothing better could be found to meet the requirements of this issue than the charge of Judge Kane, coupled with the indictment of the Grand Jury. In the light of the Emancipation and the Fifteenth Amendment, they are too transparent to need a single word of comment. Judge and jury having found the accused chargeable with Treason, nothing remained, so far as the men were concerned, but to bide their time as best they could in prison. Most of them were married, and had wives and children clinging to them in this hour of fearful looking for of judgment.

THE LAW OF TREASON, AS LAID DOWN BY JUDGE KANE

The following charge to the Grand Jury of the United States District Court, in reference to the Slave-hunting affray in Lancaster county, and preparatory to their finding bills of indictment against the prisoners, was delivered on Monday, September 28, by Judge Kane:

"Gentlemen of the Grand Jury:—It has been represented to me, that since we met last, circumstances have occurred in one of the neighboring counties in our District, which should call for your prompt scrutiny, and perhaps for the energetic action of the Court. It is said that a citizen of the State of Maryland, who had come into Pennsylvania to reclaim a fugitive from labor, was forcibly obstructed in the attempt by a body of armed men, assaulted, beaten and murdered; that some members of his family, who had accompanied him in the pursuit, were at the same time, and by the same party, maltreated and grievously wounded; and that an officer of justice, constituted under the authority of this Court, who sought to arrest the fugitive, was impeded and repelled by menaces and violence, while proclaiming his character, and exhibiting his warrant. It is said, too, that the time and manner of these outrages, their asserted object, the denunciations by which they were preceded, and the simultaneous action of most of the guilty parties, evinced a combined purpose forcibly to resist and make nugatory a constitutional provision and the statutes enacted in pursuance of it: and it is added, in confirmation of this, that for some months back, gatherings of people, strangers, as well as citizens, have been held from time to time in the vicinity of the place of the recent outbreaks, at which exhortations were made and pledges interchanged to hold the law for the recovery of fugitive slaves as of no validity, and to defy its execution. Such are some of the representations that have been made in my hearing, and in regard to which, it has become your duty, as the Grand Inquest of the District, to make legal inquiry. Personally, I know nothing of the facts, or the evidence relating to them. As a member of the Court, before which the accused persons may hereafter be arraigned and tried, I have sought to keep my mind altogether free from any impressions of their guilt or innocence, and even from an extra judicial knowledge of the circumstances which must determine the legal character of the offence that has thus been perpetrated. It is due to the great interests of public justice, no less than to the parties implicated in a criminal charge, that their cause should be in no wise and in no degree prejudged. And in referring, therefore, to the representations which have been made to me, I have no other object than to point you to the reasons for my addressing you at this advanced period of our sessions, and to enable you to apply with more facility and certainty the principles and rules of law, which I shall proceed to lay before you.

If the circumstances, to which I have adverted, have in fact taken place, they involve the highest crime known to our laws. Treason against the United States is defined by the Constitution, Art. 3, Sec. 3, cl. 1, to consist in "levying war against them, or adhering to their enemies, giving them aid and comfort." This definition is borrowed from the ancient Law of England, Stat. 25, Edw. 3, Stat. 5, Chap. 2, and its terms must be understood, of course, in the sense which they bore in that law, and which obtained here when the Constitution was adopted. The expression "levying war," so regarded, embraces not merely the act of formal or declared war, but any combination forcibly to prevent or oppose the execution or enforcement of a provision of the Constitution, or of a public Statute, if accompanied or followed by an act of forcible opposition in pursuance of such combination. This, in substance, has been the interpretation given to these words by the English Judges, and it has been uniformly and fully recognized and adopted in the Courts of the United States. (See Foster, Hale, and Hawkins, and the opinions of Iredell, Patterson, Chase, Marshall, and Washington, J. J., of the Supreme Court, and of Peters, D. J., in U. S. vs. Vijol, U. S. vs. Mitchell, U. S. vs. Fries, U. S. vs. Bollman and Swartwout, and U. S. vs. Burr.)

The definition, as you will observe, includes two particulars, both of them indispensable elements of the offence. There must have been a combination or conspiring together to oppose the law by force, and some actual force must have been exerted, or the crime of treason is not consummated. The highest, or at least the direct proof of the combination, may be found in the declared purposes of the individual party before the actual outbreak; or it may be derived from the proceedings of meetings, in which he took part openly; or which he either prompted, or made effective by his countenance or sanction,—commending, counselling and instigating forcible resistance to the law. I speak, of course, of a conspiring to resist a law, not the more limited purpose to violate it, or to prevent its application and enforcement in a particular case, or against a particular individual. The combination must be directed against the law itself. But such direct proof of this element of the offence is not legally necessary to establish its existence. The concert of purpose may be deduced from the concerted action itself, or it may be inferred from facts occurring at the time, or afterwards, as well as before.

Besides this, there must be some act of violence as the result or consequence of the combining.

But here again, it is not necessary to prove that the individual accused was a direct, personal actor in the violence. If he was present, directing, aiding, abetting, counselling, or countenancing it, he is in law guilty of the forcible act. Nor is even his personal presence indispensable. Though he be absent at the time of its actual perpetration, yet, if he directed the act, devised, or knowingly furnished the means for carrying it into effect, instigated others to perform it, he shares their guilt.

In treason there are no accessories. There has been, I fear, an erroneous impression on this subject, among a portion of our people. If it has been thought safe, to counsel and instigate others to acts of forcible oppugnation to the provisions of a statute, to inflame the minds of the ignorant by appeals to passion, and denunciations of the law as oppressive, unjust, revolting to the conscience, and not binding on the actions of men, to represent the constitution of the land as a compact of iniquity, which it were meritorious to violate or subvert, the mistake has been a grievous one; and they who have fallen into it may rejoice, if peradventure their appeals and their counsels have been hitherto without effect. The supremacy of the constitution, in all its provisions, is at the very basis of our existence as a nation. He, whose conscience, or whose theories of political or individual right, forbid him to support and maintain it in its fullest integrity, may relieve himself from the duties of citizenship, by divesting himself of its rights. But while he remains within our borders, he is to remember that successfully to instigate treason is to commit it. I shall not be supposed to imply in these remarks that I have doubts of the law-abiding character of our people. No one can know them well, without the most entire reliance on their fidelity to the constitution. Some of them may differ from the mass, as to the rightfulness or the wisdom of this or the other provision that is found in the federal compact, they may be divided in sentiment as to the policy of a particular statute, or of some provision in a statute; but it is their honest purpose to stand by the engagements, all the engagements, which bind them to their brethren of the other States. They have but one country; they recognize no law of higher social obligation than its constitution and the laws made in pursuance of it; they recognize no higher appeal than to the tribunals it has appointed; they cherish no patriotism that looks beyond the union of the States. That there are men here, as elsewhere, whom a misguided zeal impels to violations of law; that there are others who are controlled by false sympathies, and some who yield too readily and too fully to sympathies not always false, or if false, yet pardonable, and become criminal by yielding, that we have, not only in our jails and alms houses, but segregated here and there in detached portions of the State, ignorant men, many of them without political rights, degraded in social position, and instinctive of revolt, all this is true. It is proved by the daily record of our police courts, and by the ineffective labors of those good men among us, who seek to detach want from temptation, passion from violence, and ignorance from crime.

But it should not be supposed that any of these represent the sentiment of Pennsylvania, and it would be to wrong our people sorely, to include them in the same category of personal, social, or political morals. It is declared in the article of the Constitution, which I have already cited, that 'no person shall be convicted of treason, unless on the testimony of two witnesses to the same overt act, or on confession in open court.' This and the corresponding language in the act of Congress of the 30th of April, 1790, seem to refer to the proofs on the trial, and not to the preliminary hearing before the committing magistrate, or the proceeding before the grand inquest. There can be no conviction until after arraignment on bill found. The previous action in the case is not a trial, and cannot convict, whatever be the evidence or the number of witnesses. I understand this to have been the opinion entertained by Chief Justice Marshall, 1 Burr's Trial, 195, and though it differs from that expressed by Judge Iredell on the indictment of Fries (1 Whart. Am. St. Tr. 480), I feel authorized to recommend it to you, as within the terms of the Constitution, and involving no injustice to the accused. I have only to add that treason against the United States may be committed by any one resident or sojourning within its territory, and under the protection of its laws, whether he be a citizen or an alien. (Fost. C. L. 183, 5.—1 Hale 59, 60, 62. 1 Hawk. ch. 17, § 5, Kel. 38.)

Besides the crime of treason, which I have thus noticed, there are offences of minor grades, against the Constitution and the State, some or other of which may be apparently established by the evidence that will come before you.

These are embraced in the act of Congress, on the 30th of Sept., 1790, Ch. 9, Sac. 22, on the subject of obstructing or resisting the service of legal process,—the act of the 2d of March, 1831, Chap. 99, Sec. 2, which secures the jurors, witnesses, and officers of our Courts in the fearless, free, and impartial administration of their respective functions,—and the act of the 18th of September, 1850, Ch. 60, which relates more particularly to the rescue, or attempted rescue, of a fugitive from labor. These Acts were made the subject of a charge to the Grand Jury of this Court in November last, of which I shall direct a copy to be laid before you; and I do not deem it necessary to repeat their provisions at this time.

Gentlemen of the Grand Jury: You are about to enter upon a most grave and momentous duty. You will be careful in performing it, not to permit your indignation against crime, or your just appreciation of its perilous consequences, to influence your judgment of the guilt of those who may be charged before you with its commission. But you will be careful, also, that no misguided charity shall persuade you to withhold the guilty from the retributions of justice. You will inquire whether an offence has been committed, what was its legal character, and who were the offenders,—and this done, and this only, you will make your presentments according to the evidence and the law. Your inquiries will not be restricted to the conduct of the people belonging to our own State. If in the progress of them, you shall find that men have been among us, who, under whatever mask of conscience or of peace, have labored to incite others to treasonable violence, and who, after arranging the elements of the mischief, have withdrawn themselves to await the explosion they had contrived, you will feel yourselves bound to present the fact to the Court,—and however distant may be the place in which the offenders may have sought refuge, we give you the pledge of the law, that its far-reaching energies shall be exerted to bring them up for trial,—if guilty, to punishment. The offence of treason is not triable in this Court; but by an act of Congress, passed on the 8th of August, 1845, Chap. 98, it is made lawful for the Grand Jury, empanelled and sworn in the District Court, to take cognizance of all the indictments for crimes against the United States within the jurisdiction of either of the Federal Courts of the District. There being no Grand Jury in attendance at this time in the Circuit Court to pass upon the accusations I have referred to in the first instance, it has fallen to my lot to assume the responsible office of expounding to you the law in regard to them. I have the satisfaction of knowing that if the views I have expressed are in any respect erroneous, they must undergo the revision of my learned brother of the Supreme Court, who presides in this Circuit, before they can operate to the serious prejudice of any one; and that if they are doubtful even, provision exists for their re-examination in the highest tribunal of the country."

On the strength of Judge Kane's carefully-drawn up charge, the Grand Jury found true bills of indictment against forty of the Christiana offenders charged with treason. James Jackson, an aged member of the Society of Friends (a Quaker), and a well-known non-resistant abolitionist, was of this number. With his name the blanks were filled up; the same form (with regard to these bills) was employed in the case of each one of the accused.

The following is a COPY OF THE INDICTMENT.

Eastern District of Pennsylvania, ss.:

The Grand Inquest of the United States of America, inquiring for the Eastern District of Pennsylvania, on their oaths and affirmations, respectfully do present that James Jackson, yeoman of the District aforesaid, owing allegiance to the United States of America, wickedly devising and intending the peace and tranquility of said United States to disturb, and prevent the execution of the laws thereof within the same, to wit, a law of the United States entitled "An act respecting fugitives from justice and persons escaping from the service of their masters," approved February twelfth, one thousand seven hundred and ninety-three, and also a law of the United States entitled "An act to amend, and supplementary to the act entitled, An act respecting fugitives from justice and persons escaping from the service of their masters, approved February the twelfth, one thousand seven hundred and ninety-three," which latter supplementary act was approved September eighteenth, one thousand eight hundred and fifty, on the eleventh day of September, in the year of our Lord, one thousand eight hundred and fifty-one, in the county of Lancaster, in the State of Pennsylvania and District aforesaid, and within the jurisdiction of this Court, wickedly and traitorously did intend to levy war against the United States within the same. And to fulfill and bring to effect the said traitorous intention of him, the said James Jackson, he, the said James Jackson afterward, to wit, on the day and year aforesaid, in the State, District and County aforesaid, and within the jurisdiction of this Court, with a great multitude of persons, whose names, to this Inquest are as yet unknown, to a great number, to wit, to the number of one hundred persons and upwards, armed and arrayed in a war-like manner, that is to say, with guns, swords, and other warlike weapons, as well offensive as defensive, being then and there unlawfully and traitorously assembled, did traitorously assemble and combine against the said United States, and then and there, with force and arms, wickedly and traitorously, and with the wicked and traitorous intention to oppose and prevent, by means of intimidation and violence, the execution of the said laws of the United States within the same, did array and dispose themselves in a war like and hostile manner against the said United States, and then and there, with force and arms, in pursuance of such their traitorous intention, he, the said James Jackson, with the said persons so as aforesaid, wickedly and traitorously did levy war against the United States. And further, to fulfill and bring to effect the said traitorous intention of him, the said James Jackson, and in pursuance and in execution of the said wicked and traitorous combination to oppose, resist and prevent the said laws of the United States from being carried into execution, he, the said James Jackson, afterwards, to wit, on the day and year first aforesaid, in the State, District and county aforesaid, and within the jurisdiction aforesaid, with the said persons whose names to this Inquest are as yet unknown, did, wickedly and traitorously assemble against the said United States, with the avowed intention by force of arms and intimidation to prevent the execution of the said laws of the United States within the same; and in pursuance and execution of such their wicked and traitorous combination, he, the said James Jackson, then and there with force and arms, with the said persons to a great number, to wit, the number of one hundred persons and upwards, armed and arrayed in a warlike manner, that is to say, with guns, swords, and other warlike weapons, as well offensive as defensive, being then and there, unlawfully and traitorously assembled, did wickedly, knowingly, and traitorously resist and oppose one Henry H. Kline, an officer, duly appointed by Edward D. Ingraham, Esq., a commissioner, duly appointed by the Circuit Court of the United States, for the said district, in the execution of the duty of the office of the said Kline, he, the said Kline, being appointed by the said Edward Ingraham, Esq., by writing under his hand, to execute warrants and other process issued by him, the said Ingraham, in the performance of his duties as Commissioner, under the said laws of the United States, and then and there, with force and arms, with the said great multitude of persons, so as, aforesaid, unlawfully and traitorously assembled, and armed and arrayed in manner as aforesaid, he, the said, James Jackson, wickedly and traitorously did oppose and resist, and prevent the said Kline from executing the lawful process to him directed and delivered by the said commissioner against sundry persons, then residents of said county, who had been legally charged before the said commissioner as being persons held to service or labor in the State of Maryland, and owing such service or labor to a certain Edward Gorsuch, under the laws of the said State of Maryland, had escaped therefrom, into the said Eastern district of Pennsylvania; which process, duly issued by the said commissioner, the said Kline then and there had in his possession, and was then and there proceeding to execute, as by law he was bound to do; and so the grand inquest, upon their respective oaths and affirmations aforesaid, do say, that the said James Jackson, in manner aforesaid, as much as in him lay, wickedly and traitorously did prevent, by means of force and intimidation, the execution of the said laws of the United States, in the said State and District. And further, to fulfill and bring to effect, the said traitorous intention of him, the said James Jackson, and in further pursuance, and in the execution of the said wicked and traitorous combination to expose, resist, and prevent the execution of the said laws of the said United States, in the State and District aforesaid, he, the said James Jackson, afterwards, to wit, on the day and year first aforesaid, in the State, county, and district aforesaid, and within the jurisdiction of this court, with the said persons whose names to the grand inquest aforesaid, are as yet unknown, did, wickedly and traitorously assemble against the said United States with the avowed intention, by means of force and intimidation, to prevent the execution of the said laws of the United Suites in the State and district aforesaid, and in pursuance and execution of such, their wicked and traitorous combination and intention, then and there to the State, district, and county aforesaid, and within the jurisdiction of this court, with force and arms, with a great multitude of persons, to wit, the number of one hundred persons and upwards, armed and arrayed in a warlike manner, that is to say, with guns, swords, and other warlike weapons, as well offensive as defensive, being then and there unlawfully and traitorously assembled, he, the said James Jackson, did, knowingly, and unlawfully assault the said Henry H. Kline, he, the said Kline, being an officer appointed by writing, under the hand of the said Edward D. Ingraham, Esq., a commissioner under said laws, to execute warrants and other process, issued by the said commissioner in the performance of his duties as such; and he, the said James Jackson, did, then and there, traitorously, with force and arms, against the will of the said

Kline, liberate and take out of his custody, persons by him before that time arrested, and in his lawful custody, then and there being, by virtue of lawful process against them issued by the said commissioner, they being legally charged with being persons held to service or labor in the State of Maryland, and owing such service or labor to a certain Edward Gorsuch, under the laws of the said State of Maryland, who had escaped therefrom into the said district; and so the grand inquest aforesaid, upon their oaths and affirmations, afore said, do say, that he, the said James Jackson, as much as in him lay, did, then and there, in pursuance and in execution of the said wicked and traitorous combination and intention, wickedly and traitorously, by means of force and intimidation, prevent the execution of the said laws of the United States, in the said State and district.

And further to fulfill and bring to effect the said traitorous intention of him, the said James Jackson, and in pursuance and in execution of the said wicked and traitorous combination to oppose, resist and prevent the said laws of the United States from being carried into execution, he, the said James Jackson, afterwards, to wit, on the day and year first aforesaid, and on divers other days, both before and afterwards in the State and district aforesaid, and within the jurisdiction of this court, with the said persons to this inquest as yet unknown, maliciously and traitorously did meet, conspire, consult, and agree among themselves, further to oppose, resist, and prevent, by means of force and intimidation, the execution of the said laws herein before specified.

And further to fulfill, perfect, and bring to effect the said traitorous intention of him the said James Jackson, and in pursuance and execution of the said wicked and traitorous combination to oppose and resist the said laws of the United States from being carried into execution, in the State and district aforesaid, he, the said James Jackson, together with the other persons whose names are to this inquest as yet unknown, on the day and year first afore said, and on divers other days and times, as well before and after, at the district aforesaid, within the jurisdiction of said court, with force and arms, maliciously and traitorously did prepare and compose, and did then and there maliciously and traitorously cause and procure to be prepared and composed, divers books, pamphlets, letters, declarations, resolutions, addresses, papers and writings, and did then and there maliciously and traitorously publish and disperse and cause to be published and dispersed, divers other books and pamphlets, letters, declarations, resolutions, addresses, papers and writings; the said books, pamphlets, letters, declarations, resolutions, addresses, papers and writings, so respectively prepared, composed, published and dispersed, as last aforesaid, containing therein, amongst other things, incitements, encouragements, and exhortations, to move, induce and persuade persons held to service in any of the United States, by the laws thereof, who had escaped into the said district, as well as other persons, citizens of said district, to resist, oppose, and prevent, by violence and intimidation, the execution of the said laws, and also containing therein, instructions and directions how and upon what occasion, the traitorous purposes last aforesaid, should and might be carried into effect, contrary to the form of the act of Congress in such case made and provided, and against the peace and dignity of the United States.

> John W. Ashmead,
> Attorney of the U. S. for the Eastern
> District of Pennsylvania

The abolitionists were leaving no stone unturned in order to triumphantly meet the case in Court. During the interim, many tokens of kindness and marks of Christian benevolence were extended to the prisoners by their friends and sympathizers; among these none deserve more honorable mention than the noble act of Thomas L. Kane (son of Judge Kane, and now General), in tendering all the prisoners a sumptuous Thanksgiving dinner, consisting of turkey, etc., pound cake, etc., etc. The dinner for the white prisoners, Messrs. Hanaway, Davis, and Scarlett, was served in appropriate style in the room of Mr. Morrison, one of the keepers. The U. S. Marshal, A. E. Roberts, Esq., several of the keepers, and Mr. Hanes, one of the prison officers, dined with the prisoners as their guests. Mayor Charles Gilpin was also present and accepted an invitation to test the quality of the luxuries, thus significantly indicating that he was not the enemy of Freedom.

Mrs. Martha Hanaway, the wife of the "traitor" of that name, and who had spent most of her time with her husband since his incarceration, served each of the twenty-seven colored "traitors" with a plate of the delicacies, and the supply being greater than the demand, the balance was served to outsiders in other cells on the same corridor.

The pro-slavery party were very indignant over the matter, and the Hon. Mr. Brent thought it incumbent upon him to bring this high-handed procedure to the notice of the Court, where he received a few crumbs of sympathy, from the pro-slavery side, of course. But the dinner had been so handsomely arranged, and coming from the source that it did, it had a very telling effect. Long

189

before this, however, Mr. T. L. Kane had given abundant evidence that he approved of the Underground Rail Road, and was a decided opponent of the Fugitive Slave Law; in short, that he believed in freedom for all men, irrespective of race or color.

Castner Hanaway was first to be tried; over him, therefore, the great contest was to be made. For the defence of this particular case, the abolitionists selected J. M. Read, Thaddeus Stevens, Joseph S. Lewis and Theodore Cuyler, Esqs. On the side of the Fugitive Slave Law, and against the "traitors," were U. S. District Attorney, John W. Ashmead, Hon. James Cooper, James R. Ludlow, Esq., and Robert G. Brent, Attorney General of Maryland. Mr. Brent was allowed to act as "overseer" in conducting matters on the side of the Fugitive Slave Law. On this infamous enactment, combined with a corrupted popular sentiment, the pro-slavery side depended for success. The abolitionists viewed matters in the light of freedom and humanity, and hopefully relied upon the justice of their cause and the power of truth to overcome and swallow up all the Pharaoh's rods of serpents as fast as they might be thrown down.

The prisoners having lain in their cells nearly three months, the time for their trial arrived. Monday morning, November 24th, the contest began. The first three days were occupied in procuring jurors. The pro-slavery side desired none but such as believed in the Fugitive Slave Law and in "Treason" as expounded in the Judge's charge and the finding of the Grand Jury.

The counsel for the "Traitors" carefully weighed the jurors, and when found wanting challenged them; in so doing, they managed to get rid of most all of that special class upon whom the prosecution depended for a conviction. The jury having been sworn in, the battle commenced in good earnest, and continued unabated for nearly two weeks. It is needless to say, that the examinations and arguments would fill volumes, and were of the most deeply interesting nature.

No attempt can here be made to recite the particulars of the trial other than by a mere reference. It was, doubtless, the most important trial that ever took place in this country relative to the Underground Rail Road passengers, and in its results more good was brought out of evil than can easily be estimated. The pro-slavery theories of treason were utterly demolished, and not a particle of room was left the advocates of the peculiar institution to hope, that slave-hunters in future, in quest of fugitives, would be any more safe than Gorsuch. The tide of public sentiment changed—Hanaway, and the other "traitors," began to be looked upon as having been greatly injured, and justly entitled to public sympathy and honor, while confusion of face, disappointment and chagrin were plainly visible throughout the demoralized ranks of the enemy. Hanaway was victorious.

An effort was next made to convict Thompson, one of the colored "traitors." To defend the colored prisoners, the old Abolition Society had retained Thaddeus Stevens, David Paul Brown, William S. Peirce, and Robert P. Kane, Esqs. (son of Judge Kane). Stevens, Brown and Peirce were well-known veterans, defenders of the slave wherever and whenever called upon so to do. In the present case, they were prepared for a gallant stand and a long siege against opposing forces. Likewise, R. P. Kane, Esq., although a young volunteer in the anti-slavery war, brought to the work great zeal, high attainments, large sympathy and true pluck, while, in view of all the circumstances, the committee of arrangements felt very much gratified to have him in their ranks.

By this time, however, the sandy foundations of "over-seer" Brent and Co. (on the part of slavery), had been so completely swept away by the Hon. J. M. Read and Co., on the side of freedom, that there was but little chance left to deal heavy blows upon the defeated advocates of the Fugitive Slave Law. Thompson was pronounced "not guilty." The other prisoners, of course, shared the same good luck. The victory was then complete, equally as much so as at Christiana. Underground Rail Road stock arose rapidly, and a feeling of universal rejoicing pervaded the friends of freedom from one end of the country to the other.

Especially were slave-holders taught the wholesome lesson, that the Fugitive Slave Law was no guarantee against "red hot shot," nor the charges of U. S. Judges and the findings of Grand Juries, together with the superior learning of counsel from slave-holding Maryland, any guarantee that "traitors" would be hung. In every respect, the Underground Rail Road made capital by the treason. Slave-holders from Maryland especially were far less disposed to hunt their runaway property than they had hitherto been. The Deputy Marshal likewise considered the business of catching slaves very unsafe.

JAMES PENNY BOYD

The author of this biography of William Still, James Penny Boyd, was born in Fairfield, Lancaster County, Pennsylvania, to Mr. and Mrs. William Thomas Boyd on December 20, 1836. James entered Lafayette College in the fall of 1855 and graduated four years later as valedictorian, distinguishing himself as a Greek scholar while being awarded a degree of Doctor of Laws. James studied law in the office of Isaac Heister in Lancaster. Soon after passing the Lancaster bar, he traveled to Washington, D.C., and obtained a position as private secretary to Thaddeus Stephens, from whom James no doubt learned about the plight of African Americans. Boyd's work with Stephens placed him at the forefront of congressional reconstruction legislation and in the impeachment proceedings against President Andrew Johnson. After leaving Stephens, James expanded his professional activities, becoming an author, historian, editor, and a lawyer. Following the Civil War, Dr. Boyd embraced close friendships with future United States presidents Ulysses S. Grant and William McKinley. For the first 30 years of the postbellum period, Boyd maintained law offices in Philadelphia and Washington, D.C. From his Philadelphia office, Boyd served as the civil lawyer of the United States government and became associated with many prominent men, who considered James a leader in every public movement at that time. Despite his very active public and professional life, James found the time to author biographies of Grant, McKinley, James G. Blaine and Genl. William T. Sherman. His other writings include *The Building and Ruling of the Republic, The History of the Indian Wars, Stanley in Africa, Red Men on the Warpath*, and several Greek textbooks. He was a life member of the Historical Publishing Society. During the early 1880s, he served as editor of the *Philadelphia Press*, a daily newspaper published in its namesake. In 1896 Oxford University conferred on James P. Boyd an honorary Doctor of Laws, a distinction awarded to few Americans at that time. James married Alice Elizabeth Heckert, daughter of Francis Heckert, who owned the *Lancaster Examiner* newspaper for many years. James's wife died in 1900 and he spent the final year of his life living with his daughter, Alice, in Scranton, Pennsylvania. He continued with his literary work until a week before his death, although he began failing three months earlier. One obituary noted, "He was the owner of the library which had few equals in this state [Pennsylvania]. He knew his books and he made them his companions." James Penny Boyd died on December 2, 1910 at 5:45 p.m. His body traveled to Philadelphia by train with the funeral held in that city on December 5, 1910.

Paul W. Schopp

Index

Colophon

The text of this edition was first edited, designed, and typeset by Maria Armstrong and Lindsay S. Ferrigno. Publication was supervised by Tom Kinsella and Paul W. Schopp. Thanks to Samuel Still for his foreword.

The text is set in 12- and 11-point Adobe Garamond Pro. Pagination does not follow the original edition, but original spelling is retained throughout. Punctuation has been lightly modernized. Cover design by SJCHC.

South Jersey Culture & History Center

Our Mission

The mission of the South Jersey Culture & History Center is to help foster awareness within local communities of the rich cultural and historical heritage of southern New Jersey, to promote the study of this heritage, especially among area students, and to produce publishable materials that provide a lasting and deepened understanding of this heritage.

www.ingramcontent.com/pod-product-compliance
Lightning Source LLC
LaVergne TN
LVHW091216080426
835509LV00009B/1030